THE WILL OF EROS

Selected Poems 1930-1970

PARKER TYLER

BLACK SPARROW PRESS • LOS ANGELES • 1972

Grateful acknowledgement is made to Bern Porter
for permission to reprint *The Granite Butterfly*, to
the Press of James A. Decker for the poems from
The Metaphor in the Jungle, and to the following
publications where some of these poems originally
appeared: Accent, Compass, Contact, Exiles An-
thology, The Nation, New Directions Anthology,
New Mexico Quarterly Review, Pagany, Partisan
Review, Poetry, and Seven.

Black Sparrow Press
P.O. Box 25603
Los Angeles, California
90025

Table of Contents

THE METAPHOR IN THE JUNGLE

This book is for Charles Boultenhouse

TESTAMENT FROM THE INHERITORS OF
THE WASTE LAND

While we drop our consonants
The actor remembers and rehearses his lines
He remembers to remember the emphasis
We remember the emphasis
We forget to remember the rehearsal

The actor must remember the hour
Of the rehearsal, he must be
In an Eliot-hurry. We
Must not be in an Eliot-hurry.
We must remember our dignity.

Our dignity is not the actor's dignity
The saving of us from embarrassment
The triumph of the learned syllable
Echoing like a bell;
This is not the breath of our satisfaction
The uptake of our pleasure

We are dwellers in leisure.
Our word is Mallarmé's swan
Undivided in feather and
Unrehearsed in movement
We do not remove our feathers
After the performance. We keep them.

We do not go to the Night Club
After the performance
In order to relax after our triumph
Or to listen to the rehearsals
Of our triumph. We do

Not go to the bar of drinking
Except to drink, nor go to the bar
Of thinking except to think.

The actor arrives at his pay-check
And the Elusive Thing called Fame
And he rehearses the fame every morning
That we rehearse the blame
We rehearse the blame yet we seize the lights
We rehearse the phosphene-spots, and
On the inside of the fallen lids
Of our expert-dreamer's eyes,
None is that hero that dies
In the violet spot.

There is something we do
That is called Nothing that the actor
Does not do. Something that within the Plot
Of time we do not plot. We are the unplotters
Unstringers. We grasp the scissors
From the palsied hand and we unscissor
And we deflower the dropped forgotten flower
That the stagehand fingers for a moment, then puts back.

There is nothing we have to say that
We do not lean over saying as
From a balcony, there is no balcony of words
We do not drop voice from as
From the murmurous one of Juliet
Sounding and unhinged from sound

Ah, honeysweet Romeo might be intercepted
By absence of that elocutionary sound

The night is a bouquet of a strange delay
And the day an instant of impetuous waiting
Cool and deliberate as a fan.
If we are monsters yet we have not masks
But naked stalk the naked idea love
If we do not love the way Time the actor loves,
Under a sun of summer sumptuousness
We grow irrevocably, simply, tan.

We remember our inadequacy in our parts
Rather than our adequacy—
But we forget our inadequacy
As we forget our adequacy
In straining over the footlights of
Our brows. We abhor the nights
As an actor loves his "post-mortems."
We abhor the sleepless nights
As an actor sleeps in the "post-mortems."

THE METAPHOR IN THE JUNGLE

As the squid reflects
And yields to the ultimate
As steps the stepper
In the thick hood of fear
In the slack cape of love
In the pause that runs
That is still with flight
As continuous and craving
Turns mouth on mouth
Snarling and kissing
Or kissing and licking
As the flatcheeked cobra
And the ribbony king snake
Lie down and whisper
Of Europe and Asia
As they loll in Africa
And transfix America
As under the flying
Falcon the decorative
Dead swirls to a fetid
Immortality as the
Bee ceases to buzz
Lying flat on its back
And flush to the captor
Is sucked of its honey
As again the mantis
Prays rears attacks
As the bitten snake
Twists out of the snake's mouth out of
The bite as the snake whips away
From the snake as the eyes of the giraffe
On the neck's slender watchtower

Sparkle and cry Danger and
Feel the weight of the tiger
Feel the weight and the claws
At the heartshaped breastbone
As the antelope screams at the
Tiger shadowing the waterhole
And the zebra at the tiger's shadow
Swerves beyond the waterhole
As silence sets in at the cheetah's
Walk and clamor is built by the bison's
Shoulder the metaphor in its lair
Is animal: a rioting at twilight
Insatiate outrageous and sudden

And we are startled by the prowling metaphor
By the long death racing through the thicket
Bluff of incisor and delicate of blow
Deadly or lovely and pashing or pausing
Before the wide swallow: startled as the
Riven plants of the jungle are startled
Having to unseal and seal their leaves
Rocked to the roots by the trespasser
Having to leave and come back to their leaves
Sliced by the rampage of the burning leaper
O metaphor it was thy hand was caught
Drawing from the womb of grass the fleet
Tiger glutted and wet on the furry pauses
And painted the strawberry-colored yawn

As we writhe out of the tightening debt
As we jerk shamed from the flat jaw of
The lurking beggar and as we dodge

13

The roving tooth of the class-struggle
Fly madly on our dripping wings the
Worm of lust erect in our beaks
As we place at the throat of desire
Sleep's diminutive darling dagger
The metaphor comes like a shadow
From dense jungle we open the wound
Of the elephant obsessed with the female
We lie with the kangaroo lovely on childbed
Rehearse with the Grandmother Ape at dusk
The blond movements of the diaper folders

Have we not burning brooding and burning
Flaked our skins about us to the ankles
Wondering jumped toward her and recoiled
Landed on fur of her hair and on new
Velvet of her skin and slipped moaning
To a sitting posture and seen trickle
The slow uncriminal speech weaving
The red metaphor from her voiceless thighs?
Heard young snore of the sleeping plunderer
The thunderous fists of the curled singer?

As the crawl crossed with the crawl
On the forgotten slope of slime
As the crab ate with the non-crab
And ate the non-crab and courted
The super-crab and was mated and eaten
And crossed and crossed again
Over the star-crossed couple
The branch with the locking branch
As from the powdery bough of green

The marble-eyed the lynx
Leaned down and sighed later
Bearing away a burdened stomach:
Juliet Juliet! thy grace from the lifted
Stone slid and brought home
Meat for the muted in the fern and
Romeo reached and was nape-master

As we strive and have striven
From the elk's brow and dream
Of broken flesh (as he) we have dreamed
And dream now of poised air
And of aërial pose as the elk
Bows his head for the charge and charges
And is gored by the duplicate horns
And sinks to his knees and
Strives shaking his horns
The metaphors strive: their hurled brows
Proud as plutocracies and they have striven
For their plutocracies shaking on their knees
Have striven horn against horn: smoke
Of the snout amidst smoke of the snout

But we have never dared digest dared forage
And grow fat as Marx in his lair quivered
To bring forth something to snatch
Something from the snapping jaws
As Marx stood up from the cribclothes
And walked from the squealing myth
Soaked in the sweat of seeing the hallucinate
Animal drinking at the historic pool

15

But I have seen rear
And convulse and re-convulse
The intransigent metaphor
At the cue of repose: rear
And extend
Its claw of loveliness
Restless
As the heart in the mouth of midnight
By the clock's teeth snared and entranced
Uncertain and watchful as a child
In the middle of a circle
I lie straight and curl
Coquetting: coquette with the bird
Crowing in the crooked straw: burst
Into the barnyard greeting
Ever ever the ruff frenetic the
Repetition and the recapitulation
Flirt with the feeler of the fawning
Octopus: select my favorite and turn
Tossing between blacknesses and
Provoke my favorite: flaunting
My odor opening, and

As the slipper in the sea evades
As the fish frozen in the gesture of
Swimming from the sea-death slips
Easily from the past of annihilation
Into the future of sea metaphors
As the soldier dodges the bullet
As the defaulter eludes the summons
The proposed law escapes legislation
As with equal celerity and precision
They solve nothing: with equal precision

And with equal celerity the metaphor
Averts the fang of the poet and
Jubilates and is futile and free

And with equal precision and celerity
The metaphor welcomes the fang
Of the poet and is skinned and glittering
White ring and no ring final ring
Which is white visible and invisible
In the jungle ring on black ring
So in great night the metaphors
So in great night a crouching cancer
Under Adam's gleaming equine plume
And Eve the ape the resurrection
Golden and nude in the bewigged dawn

BEAU-ULYSSES-X

Harken
> deaf-eared one

appear; cursed with the wise presumption of flesh; of
> accidents to be worshipped
intrigue levitation: —
> debase usual
habit-mountains: —
> assume, assumption
course among devils to port-pouring: —

> *My Ulysses*
about whose body fatal familiars grope
> the eyes of your hair
rich in waves, your brows arched with sunsets,
> the cruelty robbed
of your emasculated breasts
> ready to receive
rosettes of fame: exploding kisses
> like stars
back-exploding to kisses;
> no Penelope wants you
or waits, spins
> anything but lethal trusts
you couldn't put leg in.
> Your home
is Never-Never Land;
> you will bend
here to tricks;
> kohl will blacken
your eyes not bruised;
> your hairs

18

not now taught will teach the abstract; —
                  electricity-libidinous: —
supernumerary rampants: —
                  anti-bourgeoisie-anti: —
damned, sybaritic gloats: —
               all
will cake your sighs, briefer than your lungs' pant!

    The Male Shining
whored in your grouping, flesh-citizen
        crammed for a dream
of beachcombers' clothes, the growth
        on the chin
changed for jasmine-scented powder in blunted pores: —

    Cupid's-bow
at stake
        above your chin: Woolworth's
becomes timeless, your moronish
loose moment, Praxiteles or bust! —
                On time!

rape-artist-nerts
            your bloom
surely yet bellodorously fills the conch of implacable Wave-Set.

                    (still waves
your hair, your mouth set for the kiss,
             Beau
Ulysses, acrobat tied to
        (my)

19

Gethsemane (the mast!)
you
atrophy in a pause time will reluctantly relieve you of;

FREUD OF ASSISI

Freud, driven to his mountain, sequestered the dim serpent
With wings, and curries the masked eagle, snowed in sorrow
Furred the deep little dove and flings on the ponderous air
Hot happy hummingbirds and soothes the vacant brown
    sparrow

Freud on his lonely mountain, breeding his beautiful birds
From sadness, patient and thoughtful is, looking at love
And the liquid exile craning his neck at love's still head
From his foreign field is happy but never is bird enough

Never is enough the lover to get around beauty's back
Nor the front of the foremost fact is near enough nor big
To rest the wing of air within time's aviary
Or lift out of space the fold of the leaf of the fig

From the faint clear room of ventilated rhyme, ah rapid
The poet's sound and sleep come quivering, cool and fine
And with angelic art seek the stoneless veering pathway
Toward spot and spangle where the doting dove will dine

Ah birdlike beasts that come at call and feed and fly
Deep from the shallow forest of the air: the côte of crime:
The slower den of dream and dirt dissolved on space
However far or fancy in the paradise of time

His symbol from the garden of the phallic fiction
Grows up in grooming and gets into space: the dress
For flying in the complex naked bed: or breeding
The peacock of consolation for the barren princess

Ah, God the breath! from head to foot the famous image
Of the inmate's story crows like a cock in the crooked straw
And points to Freud like a pigeon or falls like a falcon
On the staring patient, unsheathing again its classic claw

ODE FOR REALITY

Man moves in his circle and is silent, graces his days
With bunting, buries his love in a landslide
Of sleeping, awakes to put prayer on the hooves of hours
And falters. Goes straight to the door of the simpering demon.

Remote above history, worships a god whose nature is wild
Changeful and symmetrical, be it woman or father. O
Florescent meadows have been crossed on seeing chariots
Behind the white horses of hope, one wrought like a man.

Love is infinite, a saying ruled wise on the edge of the tongue
The boy beats the pillow and gives in, the gaping girl submits
There was a torture practised while outside the loud parade
Made innocent stamping music: it was a hot nude fable

And the hero is no longer free, but harness-hampered.
Woman thrives like a flower between rocks, immortal of hair
Only exacting the tribute, the form of the faithless angel.
Tomorrow the child bats its eyes at the forgotten incident.

Travelling the mundane reaches of space, man is whole
In a twist of the mind, a fillip of fancy: the hollow brain
Fitting the created draughtmanship, the tabulated turns
And the sweetest one is locked there: the easy bridegroom

Mothers are frantic, are hit, immolated to exile
And mighty in milk, sisters are sick shadows or roses
One dare not touch. All must be beaten from the brain but
The beauty that enters like the heroine of a bad play.

23

Like grapes that hang from the mysterious skies, war's death
Sucked by all! War flings creator on creator for nothing
Peace comes on waves, and men pity each other at violence
Of having peace like a grave, war like a bawling birth, and

Have I lost my chance at happiness because of this? Because
The brain freezes toward midnight, writes poetry toward dawn
Thinks of love as an element? The matinee-idol is helpless
Hands move on his name, rhythmically remove the ink

Man meets man. And mind embraces mind on the platform
Before the public. Even the cafeteria is public enough
And warmth of the idea next to warmth of the idea
Blossoms. The rich juice enters a limitless being

BALLAD OF THE VASE-BREAKER

When I looked at Dostoievsky's hero, "The Idiot," again,
Suddenly I was aware of desire, steeped in time, and when
I thought of the soul of that man, invisible in his body,
I felt like fainting. I have never let my eyes drop, never,

From the trail of the spirit that gathers in the flesh of man,
Stopping here, sleeping there, going in richness or weeping,
Glimpsed and unglimpsed by the traveller on other feet, yet
Seeming ever to climb vaguely, interminably, like a comet.

There on a level with the eyes, other eyes; and the brain deep
As a sleeping snake in unwanted Africas, full of blackness,
Hissing in ego yet capable of running. Alas, the outward flesh
Trembles like a mask about to be removed. "It is outrageous,"

I think, "the dreadful difference between us, the dreadful space
Separating man and man, the unfeedable unsatisfied desire
Poised on the shoulder, saddled with wings O very monstrous!"
Zeus was a bird, I've heard, and Leda was a frightened woman.

And exhausted and fulfilled by the rumor, a lover of the
Poem, I recall I've revolted; I'll bring to the lyric moment
The ruthless lips of logic, the traveller's tongue of truth:
Strike out in a ballad, resentful. I shudder, I explode to

Remember the items of the womb and the legend of sex
Making up memory; our tall, leaning look over the shoulder
And down, back into the neat voice of Freud, like a prophet's,
Into the banality of birth, its spotlessly literal room.

O heaven! my adored moron, whose fabulous liquidness
    smites me

In the belly and stays like a statue, charming as the holiest
Of loveable girls: you were puzzled by the vase so glib as to
Finish its form, as though, all being done, you might worship.

Never, you said; and I, in the heaving collective, so frantic
I stay in my room and exult in society, its promises,
Seizing the history, history of promise and that of fulfilment;
Thus I am human. Then, why, like young Muishkin, should I pity

And retire to the vulgarest of sanitariums? Or dare I,
Shall I, take my eye from such beauty? As I write it, I feel
My heart's pity for so hopeless a search. I maintain, I maintain:
The eye of my body shall fix on that sweet and immaculate

Silhouette which, finally lacking a face, uses even a skull.
I cannot love only the mortal, ever-rescued-by-dream and
Inward success of libido! No, also that wildly pathetic
Look, lurching like a beggar from Dostoievsky's pages.

I meditate: The gods were identified. Never Venus appeared
But all knew. Apollo, handsomer than the horse, never entered
That anyone had to pronounce him. They needed no shadow. And
Therefore I conclude: Only the human, the human is broken.

ODE TO HOLLYWOOD

The movie, the history of flutter and twitter, the
Voice of the bird was dumb and transformed there,
  The voice of the bird was pluralled.

The light of the person was exiled and fastened
To the dark of the person, and flowing-imaged.
  The person was broken and knitted.

The river, the fire and the libelled ocean
Roared in a voice that was coarser than nature,
  Surprising, swift and surgical.

The simple refrain of a touched paper came
Toward us like an actor from the ensemble
  For a tiny, arrogant symphony.

Now the garden of Garbo, the silver garden,
That intimate accurate moon of behavior
  Where Greta forever walks:

As children, omnivorous through time, O
We worship there: overjoyed at the
  Remoteness, the tallness.

A terrific comforting nostalgia
Unreels in us; celluloid memory invades us;
  Our flesh is unravelled by inches.

Perforce sitting like Egypt to envision Egypt,
Griffith's stage-struck Babylonia
  Once more comes near the gazer.

Gish like a lily hypnotized into life, takes
The first silent step of nearness and shuddering
    Comes closer, comes closer than

She who gave birth: so the birth of the close-up!
At a look from the camera, walls fall away from
    DeMille's white bedrooms with Gloria.

And Charlie, the most super-sensitive, who
Stumbles, ended end-up in the deathless
    Black-and-white suit of art's elegance.

Lubitsch brought lightness, the French the mature;
Shakespeare's land gave the arabesque vowel,
    Russia the esperanto iris.

More permanent than presidents, the Vampire,
Whose sin never, at worst, was venal, was Theda;
    And Pauline demolished her perils.

We have not been cheated of the mask of Venus,
Marlene, for a thousand nights and one; and Bette,
    Jitterbug of tragediennes, lives.

The millimeter has come to the library,
To the memorial of esthetics: the museum;
    The medal of continuous hushed honor.

And now comes the magic of Lumière in
A snug dream of a theatre, the silliness and
    Wonder of old reflections.

Look there, at the face of Rudolph hugging
The heaven of wives; perhaps the bridegroom at last cometh
    Unto the shamed hell of husbands!

We can learn how futile it is in nature
To imitate the mind, whose perpetual life is
    Rewinding, and springing, and blurring . . .

Still, forever from that city of incredibly
Rapid and beautiful and fragile movement,
    The kiss in perpetuum mobile!

THE EROTICS

    The location
Of the lone dark room from which they struggle forever is
Hidden, humming, hammered to the earthquake, menacing
    The lovers

Whose homes are heated, anchored. The erotics are white heavers
And squirters, black blisterers and purpling contagions.

    The whore
And the richest roué, the social criminal, are better
Than evil and worse than good, they are the crucified,
    The artists

Whose content is sex, whose forms are theatrically
False and winsome, bitter, all clotted with fought fevers.

    The woman
And the man begin single, double everything and murder
The double, hate repetition, always love the same with
    The oath.

"I take thee" is given grown in a blurring of kiss, ended
In a brick of beauty, severed in a rose of bed: O

    The lyric
Cheating! The bride and bridegroom are stunned from winking
At coming, going; there, where it is too spacious,
    The traveller

In the erotic lands goes on elbows; back; knees; sleeping
In all but one place. The son soul-slaughtered, the mother defaced,

The uncle
Of unctuous gifts, find room for their secrets and time for
Their favorites. The mad farmer who is a weathervane for
    The actress

En route to the actor, is the truest King of the Arctic
And the lily homosexual for all his one-eyed idiocy is

    The millionaire
Erotic. Futile to shun the boast in music's sober speaking!
What? Preserve candor, proportion, the thinking ability and
    The democracy?

Yes. Erotics are feminine, bored, drinkers of the glorifiers
The glorified: curved lords of lymph, the great girls,
        lady-killers

    The man
With his moon, the priest with his paradise, the satan with
His satin, red and reversible body (alas) Heaven's
    Harry

Himself with his harp of hurt, the horsehilled hugger:
He's startlingly human, distorted as only nature

    The Platonist
In her incredible rut, her bag of broken beauties,
Distorts that she surprise us; the flirting dad, the cancers,
    The libidos,

It is so close! In looking at it we are the air it breathes
Or look so far from upper air, the forest is a scab,

The sea
A simper . . . With those, the pillow is a hand of dreaming
Fists; those sigh! reach in! stretch out and hover thick in
The images.

THE GODS

They are with nature, the underside, shaping
The babies for flags and queens; dying; raping;
        Divine quoters;

They distribute the forests, their souls paint
The honey and starve; in the end they faint
        Only. Iotas

Of evening, charmed sunsets panelling their rooms
Of death and designing, their shitten blooms,
        Their auroras,

Their opal feet and their fast rendezvous:
Shut this music together. Are the gods through
        With anima

As we are through? Seen now, from here,
The gods make a crowd. Alas, appear!
        Animus

No more? Hermaphroditus, the fused sex
Over? The question crushes. Dare we vex
        The fabulous?

Christ the bird, Ra the animal, the child
Cupid, afterward the Adult; others, wild
        As Heaven

Hunting? Whole jugular Jupiter? The volcanic
God who disappeared after issuing? The satanic
        One, even?

Thin as a page or a symbol, broad as a cry,
Icy when one is hot, and like a sigh,
      Hard featured,

They puzzle us beyond dreaming merely. Yes,
They enter unbidden the poem, confess
      Unassured.

Adonis there, and Aphrodite once,
The forms and the logic swimming. Magic suns
      And crazy

Arterial beauties: lust. Grown Apollo
Inevitable unshakable. Gone, hollow?
      We're hazy

To see, than not to see now, but we do:
Depending. O unlovely lovely Buddha: we do
      See him

Calm as a maniac. Might we be as desirous
Of their fame as they of ours; which, vaporous
      And dim,

Will hurl our flesh farther? Sit with sin or
Die erecting our shamefullest killed valor
      Without vanity?

THE PROCESS

The struggle for existence is not over,
 The struggle for existence is uncut
And is continuous and nature's veiled
 Precision is everywhere and Man's
Unveiled mistakes strive to ingratiate:
Yet the factories are correct; though they are not inspired, they go,
They conjure things from things, make clocks of crooked time.

And rhyme knits sense to sound, music
 To meaning and music to music: this
Precision is treacherous and it deserves
 Suspicion and is accused and damned
On trial (but the rhyme holds in the end).
Serene society permits these complex balances and leisure: the
Rage to spend, realize, exhaust the loadedness of all the dice.

And the nice etiquette of travel lies
 Enshrined in motion for the simplest heart;
On the face, cosmetic's still supreme.
 Though the face fail of its new effect,
The art was present when the impulse urged.
The power plant breeds in isolation like a rabbit the
City of anonymity; problems, though a million muscles are
 involved,

Stay unsolved and the suspiration
 Comes, reminds that silence is not still,
Begets the paranoiac and at dawn
 The night goes home to the bed of day
Arising to be magnificent!
History is perpetual motion, paychecks unbroken intervals,
Interests work like symphonies, processes are inward: strong.

How long (answer!) does the icebox take
    To grow too old, to haunt its humming womb?
And ghosts of automobiles go home
    To Heaven from their Cemetery. Now
Lovelier the Ford and Frigidaire!
Not only in philosophies opposites kiss, yes something glues
Minute to minute, kiss to kill and human living to human dying.

    Then sighing the machines cease, wait,
        Are listeners at last and faces of
    Existence take on naturalness, the dance
        Takes on the dancers and the unnatural
    Fertilization buds the debutante . . .
How break the rhythm? Even the wheelless dust will flower
In wheels and rings and roses, the secret process is a naught.

    Yet caught in the circular frame: gold
        Transformations enter from far time
    And seem to be. The skin under the fur,
        The brute behind the act, the god within
    The man, all burst out, are dissipated.
The magic book stands; opens; is the symbol contrived from
The transformations: the book, the statue, the crystal process,

    The progress! the miniature! the
        Illusion! the manufactured practice
    Of socialism! the mad alchemist
        Of souls and food! Houdini of
    The rent! Process does not aim, it is,
The aimless thing is cancerous, absolute, even unfamiliar;
Though at any moment, stress paraphernalia of the whore!

Yet more: for man the struggle is to add
    The wager on the racehorse to the cost
Of the party, law's deep problem to fame:
    The votes to pennies, the payable bills
To the rooms, well cleaned. Addition is all.
The mask is no matter, it is made. Even the dream is a means
For we dare not claim anything is wasted, anything left over!

THE HEROES

For Pavel Tchelitchew

Long has the pen been dropped, the sword been kissed and hung;
Long, too, the crisp vanity wilted, and laid away; long,
    The indignant words,
The individual pulse and the pulse's room, the name
And its nuance, been divided in history as in water; the
    Flaming eye suddenly

Hooded; ah! each hair stiffened at its private root; and yet,
    And yet, the dead grouped
Heroes, in their enormous vigil by the world's live body,
Have not, out of either envy or pity, lidded themselves, or sunk
    From our fickle sight!

We are flooded, this morning, with reality from a primal source;
Arising, each in his naked oneness, to receive the clothes
    Of society;
Striding, each, to his balcony, and gazing at street or field as
At nothing; half turning, allows his fingers to slide on the railing,
    Make a star of his hand.

We, subtly, dimly, growing aware of them, more alive than statues,
    An anonymous wrist
Hanging calmly, inevitably, from a magnificent nonchalant
        shoulder,
They focus us; and dimly, subtly, overwhelmingly aware of
    The news in the paper,

We think: Where on the earth does the sun not shine, and
        where, too,
Is no war done? From the top of this hill, green trees sail away

38

To the valley, and glide
To the permanent silhouette of the dimmest of waves
In the distance, clinging to that visible edge of the world
    Like our hope of peace.

Yet, since the sight itself must leap to the sky, turning backward
    To move in a single wit,
Whether I rise on the continuing curve of the cup, or recede from
Its rim, all my muscles relaxing, and return to the foot of this
    Flower-topped terrace,

It is as if those, a sun, had arisen at a signaled evolution
And with straight ray shooting from their unscattered zone,
    Eyed us, levelly,
Each hero admitted to the commodious pupil, and thus
We, the massed fighters distinct in our taut confusion,
    Are seen in a circle.

No matter how accurate our gunsight in sinking the battleship,
    It curves in their iris;
Nor how sinuous our diplomacy, it lies straight as the dead
In their hearts, though luminous. Ah, even the soldier, as he falls,
    Lies snipped like a curl!

So, miraculously, the artist may paint in an oval area
The world revolving upon itself, and reality be trapped
    Forever in a frame;
And straight by the straight railing, I am only a curving bird
Permitting my loud thoughts to soar, while those transfix me
    Even as an enemy.

39

Such a coagulation are they that, when the sunset appears,
    A diaphanous landscape,
I discern there a glitter of braid or, past the miasmic mauve
Of the sky forest, in the brilliant nudity beyond all,
    The breast of an army.

And the storm itself comes on their faces as on the face of
The landscape darkened! Then their bodies are shaken as the
                branches
    Of trees, and their faces
Congeal with the lightning, and relax with the emotions of
                thunder,
While the shadowy ceiling of the room seems a glass which
                magnifies
    Their distant eternity.

Afterward each, however, starts forward with that cry of criticism
    Which is the very self,
To silently stare at us: a world of persons in a paroxysm of living
Than the landscape more greenly, than the sky more bluely, than
    The blood more redly!

Opal of tantalization! My schedule of running and swimming
                under
The eye of those heroes fits like a jewel in the ring of this
    Radiant summer!
On what do I rely to convert the droop of my richness to brawn?
On what but those incalculable colleagues of the body,
    Its unperceived heroes?

40

Not time, nor space, nor the written myths of the blood, divide
    The phalanx of heroes;
Nor any habit or feature moulded by Plutarch, nor the finger
        of sex,
Nor the name that lives on the lips without warning or truce,
    May shuffle their stripe.

And thus, part of that indivisible landscape that clings to
Flexed muscles and kisses the crook of my arm, today's heroes
    Depend on each other;
Even as I stretch, as far on either side as I can, my belt of strength,
Their personalities equivocate, press me and taunt me
    In the gold tent of air.

This is the very same blaze surrounding each ego on earth
    Who relies for blood
On the whim of the lover. It is a vulnerable sun that thus shines
Plentifully for an instant, in time and space, on such heroes.
    Conspiracy's cloud

Is circular and slides forever over the sky of the human as
Now, climbing toward noon, I and the green landscape are subject
    To shade as to sorrow;
Even as my wish rises from the ground like an airplane to seek
A conquerable and more unified element, the single-souled heroes
    Seek their army once more.

SOCRATES

The bough has bent. The leaf is gone. The words
Have dropped to sound and sound to silences.
The noble face of Athens, like the birds
Whose flights made still the airy prophecies,
Is not, yet is, because of eternal lips
That challenged truth and that-which-goes-and-comes
And even today, like Fate, write the book that slips
Into the forms of all our vacuums.
That man who was, and is, gross and serene,
Whose naked mind outshone the very gods,
Comes with his flesh onto the fluid scene
And breathes sense in these too, too banal clods
We die with. Hemlock! what a sculptor, thou:
To build up life upon his deathward brow!

TO A PHOTOGRAPH

It is the littleness I would keep
        Of this big frail moment, or the frail
Bigness and qualitative issue of it, for
        It is a thing of lines, this amorphous
            Being that
            I would keep.

And now is set its law: as of a
        Crystal age whose masses pierce and pierce
The white depth of the page, easily
        And automatically as the
            Letters beat on,
            And the words.

The crystalline great sex: that
        Hiding behind all lighted planes, round
As a rose, whose leaf is the poem, whose
        Child is surfaces, such as this
            Snapshot, precise
            And yet blurred.

Neither can arms embrace the typewriter
        Nor, though instanter life should leave
Me, any air give birth except to breath
        Alone. But somewhere love corpuscular
            Imitates cor-
            Puscular love!

For that crook of leg, and thickness
        Of flesh, and fold of lax and simple
Tension, in those: look! is a music
        Caught and reduced, whose wild vast

Will threaten death
To kiss it all.

And did; in a way; and in more ways, when
        The light taps and the soft vents of verse
And glance's infinitesimal weight
        Of wing, stole along life's great
                Abstract curves, so
                Formless there till now.

So substanceless till now: the true sag
        And sift of monumental gaze
Theoretically having for all time's warp
        Itself to gag and give, weep on and woo,
                Muffled above, and
                Below, with ink.

Organically, I move with all my
        Named and nameless fingers, where the voice
Shows as on a map, nowhere, the single
        Sigh that delivers up, and will,
                All history's weft
                To syllabled lip.

For this, deep, would I not keep it still
        Because I could not, shallow, unless I
Statued it as statues do, but would I,
        Making all lucid, keep its loose matter-
                Of-fact mystery
                Of all frames clear,

Where, dubious at night and solemn-quick,
    The heart's eye, and the twin breasts', hug
Those paths no camera took, or ever can,
      Swallowed their own motion, and dead their rhythm:
        Immutable to rhyme,
        Impossible to scan.

CHEZ CYTHERA

Closer than hair, and of the air, air's bruit,
Its tangled troubles and its sexless hate
    Reach us, who do not wait.
Exiled automatically, sickly animal,
We ravish things and distance, but not love
    That falls, finally, from above.

Yes, finally! For it falls. Senseless our look
On it and its disguised, anonymous leaf:
    Its blind, sleeping grief.
But the breeze kisses the ear. If you don't believe
The breeze does that, die. Then you might as well:
    The god of the truth is in hell.

On the contrary, Cythera is everywhere.
That bland curl and lips, color of shadow in gold,
    Blood by the soft, crescent-fold;
Garment and stitch, bone, image of the drinking eye:
Highlighted velvet, heart staining indelibly
    All but the most frozen sky.

Extravagant simplicity and the earth!
Those laws — nudity in its endless layers,
    And a sense of being players;
An openness to that quantity, the carnal body
That snares the beast, imagination,
    Giving sensation for sensation.

Ghosts of bells . . . and of song, song's monotone . . .
A lake of illusion as high as our rhyming waists . . .
    Watteau is not to all tastes!

Well, neither is love, which is only fascination
Fastened to the most complex, laconic object: her
        Or him, vulnerable to Blur.

Prime dolls! Cythera's queen made and remade maid,
And the sacred bridegroom's exact quiddities —
        "Name, please!" — and all the oddities.
Cythera: our groan and boredom is thy little boat,
Our state of want thy license, and our lies
        Thy incomputable tax. Death's sighs:

Such puns, paradoxes like that, and the lovely
Open ground that is the orchidaceous throat
        We cram with the one silly note,
And wink, unconsciously, and sleep. Consciously.
Simply adoring beauty, holding in a hollow hand
        Fat phantoms, a cup and. . . .

SOLITAIRE

In memory of my mother

I

Into the cards goes all she has of love,
The woman who is empress of her hands:
The lone black spot she is enamored of
Sinks in the shuffling of the red, quick sands.
The mathematics of her heart is learned
As though her teacher were her history,
Whose symbols fatally are now returned
Upon the clear ground of her memory.
But she is keen here as some jeering bird
Watching for prey upon the mottled earth!
Because her heart, before, was blind-interred
Beneath the sprouting cards, she seeks the dearth
Of all the vacant air when she shall see
The bird descending on her piercingly.

II

Upon the cards she pours her wrath of blindness,
Being some faithful frenzied hawk whose wing
Hangs over the soft thing as though from kindness
But whose is the same height of shadowing.
The table's ground is now the lasting world
Whereon the fleeing dice become stone hares:
A race of frisky mockery unfurled
For the aesthetic hawk who (looking) cares . . .
But in the movement of this dotted earth
That dealt is by such accurate leaps and bounds

Runs the brave hare who is the line of mirth
Upon the grim face of a pack of hounds:
The hounds of love who make her game of skill
Too truthful and too lagging for the kill.

PRISMATIC PSYCHE

To Freud

This dream is yours! Time melts. And all the pages
Blur to a water making simple all dim sight
Starring the fabric of each fugitive night
Spent after reading: those sleeping ages
When the hero, pictured white, gluts all his rages
With doing, and does only what is right! —
Such are the icons that populate the light
Marking the soul's gold deliquescent stages.

Yet nothing, finally, but that greatest Sun,
Who is the waxing father, shall rear the dead
Illustrious deeds that weigh on us like ice;
No, nor the Noon, who is his dazzling pun,
Can fire us but in poetry, which is read
(When wide awake) by blue forgetful eyes.

NIJINSKY

The dive could come who was its fledgling first
Of wings that feathered ankles and stood up
And leapt and wide in the deep air immersed
The body that came down as soul went up
And taught the throat the foremost wind: and back
The living blood curved in the fluid hand
Whose fingers paused, and poised: the deadened slack
Was time's who stopped to see a dancer stand
Where sky was . . . There was God, where man was not
And heat in the heaving heart that moved alone
And left like a lover the still, praying spot
To surge where there were only air and bone
But once, as a mere odor comes and goes,
Dream: and the great anthropomorphic rose.

THE DROWSY MESMERIST

In memory of my father

The baby midnight in the elder brain
Cadaver is at once and parent of light
As well as the dense bellowing refrain
The ears take, partitioning out the night

And the wee hours of morning, chubby hands
Moisten, retain the universe of time —
Ah, when the doubting footprints in the sands
Ah, when the breaking booming of the chime

Form the ascetic shiftless residue!
The garment ruffled O the world's sheer piece
Between the flesh and the bright spectral view
Of that dancer in the paternal crease.

And in the surety of sexless dreams
Some horribly impossible fairy-leaf
Cradles the infant weight, settles the seams,
Prows on some hideous and sea-worn reef.

Be, therefore, be outtaken, be updrawn:
Weft of the sails and breeze of the sweet father
Leaning his face into the fists of dawn
Baring, than lashes, fierce eyes open, rather.

And then the eye-blue and the fern-like red
Of the eyeball, and jerked wind-form of the hair,
And the white of the eyeball, dark of head,
Then: the same furniture tossed anywhere.

O pace the corners dark of the love-brain
Where toys mudmuddle the white father-fact
As rabid as clock-numerals insane
Upon his changeless and unblemished tact!

This, for all midnights, is a raging wave
Eased of its tension in light-negative only:
The breast of the baby climbing from the grave
Of its dark bed it finds so deep and lonely.

So, as some whisper of the female breast
Some damp adornment of the marriage night,
Now is the full love of the dusky nest
Grown gasping to a ball of friendless fright:

Detached, and in the father's arm a ship
Blind as a bat of tears ripped from the rain:
Lull in his arms, ah the bird of the hip
Sleeps, sleeps in rigging of the big-male pain!

And as he paces out the morning hours
A father sleepless and half driven mad
The baby prunes the wide soft thunder-flowers
Caught in his father's sail to make him glad.

THE RETREAT

Come, there are ways, soul. Come to the high
Tower and the studio and watch the sky
   Infinite air
Fits like a crown on the head. Yes, it is day,
Soul, and since you care, then you will stay
   And fly, here

Where earth is a cord on the ankle and where, on wings,
Time is ranked like feathers. Something will sing
   Irregular song,
Something will sound of life, green, and from some
Other world will come crying crowds that have been
               dumb.
   And not long

You'll stay, body that breathes, pulse that glitters
On the wrist like a gem. Not all space twitters
   Soothingly, thus,
Nor always may supple vacuums take shape, or look
Neatly and spontaneously, as in this nook,
   Homogeneous.

Go, there are ways, body. Leave here the low
Vessel of humanities for the blue brow
   Of emptiness.
Then diurnity's full face (earnest as friends)
Will follow you, with a short gaze, to what ends
   Who shall confess?
   Who shall confess?

BAROQUE EPIGRAM

Ant upon ant write the text in
   The ground and the grass only of waiting
      And of the gap of gold sing silently and
         Illustrate ennui with their antennæ

And they cross out noon as in the tit-tat-toe
   Time plays with itself and it is soon
      That the absence of sound and of no-sound speaks
         And love in its veiled pure minute grows old

That sunlight wearily lies down on naked
   Buttock and pap and that grass blades
      Prepare elaborately to celebrate neglect
         And whimsies of shade spell out the label flesh

Assumes for itself wrapped tightly in a niche
   Having only the one voice unique among kinds
      Unpeeling itself to show what an artist's intent
         Soft hand requires a lifetime to find

And what is vocally named in a brief
   Polysyllable: "induplicable"
      So from estrangement comes at arm's length
         (Nappy among naps) on a new bathsheet

Its song near weeds' weave unassailably yet
   Assailably moist till the checks and stripes
      Pressed still flatter shout out a triumph
         As on their local tricolor's great fête

And with the aid of earth (abetted by eternity
      And the muscular planets) buoy up a loller
            Supine on less than a breath of what moves
                  Concealing its own hot length in the atom

Its weight and rhythmic outline stretched in
      Mysterious hesitance and cosmic bottleneck
            To throw in my eyes suddenly like soothing acid
                  Its clothed phrase and unclothed symphony

Washing them instantly of their waiting with pink
      Ablutions and drying them with cursive hairs' wit
            Till flush at the center as of bottomless space
                  A blue-sky of shadow lifts out of pink

But a few inches off! absenting itself only
      To return at once in an enormous wink
            By shifting its accent and slowly unclosing
                  Pale wings of an armpit's bruised butterfly

THREE SONNETS ON WORKS OF ART

I: LEONARDO'S "HEAD OF OUR SAVIOUR"

One can forget, amid the sunlight's burnish
And blue shadows of this image, what it is. . . .
As though the law of old myth had to furnish
Mere air with meanings, Judas with his kiss.
That-beyond-drawing tells us it is man,
That-beyond-man that it is also holy;
That-beyond-gods and Heaven's naked span
That it is beautiful . . . solely. . . .
And so . . . the soul of beauty, in whose breath,
Though shapeless first, the body forms, the face
Outfeatures, from its frame, the face of death
And lives within a world of boundless grace.
What star-streams, casual, soft, mysterious,
Can seem so far . . . and so anonymous?

II: DEGAS' "WOMAN WITH CHRYSANTHEMUMS"

For Meyer Schapiro

Each petal is a stroke — one stroke, no more —
And never did bouquet more fill a space,
In measure not so much as with her face,
She leaning elbow now, as often before,
So (hand on cheek) her richness might explore
The air, gather and tint and petal its grace
And, as from the heart's own depths, set in a vase
All the sweet flowery substances it bore.

57

Yet now the painter sees her not as she,
This pensive woman with the dreamy eyes,
Is to herself — where grows that inner soul
Sequestered from the courtship of the bee —
But in the world where men acclimatize
Women to a body, flowers to a bowl.

III: SEURAT'S "LA GRANDE JATTE"

Perhaps the artist is that monkey there,
Leashed to the large, upright, noble couple —
Petit enfant, indeed, with père and mère:
Inconspicuous, but supremely supple.
And this, this dominant light that halves the world
Is the sun's kindest finger, soft on Sunday
When the charged atoms are so passive-curled,
Bizarrely still, and nonchalant of Monday.
Life's paramount profile is a parasol:
The perky silhouettes devoid of blur;
The white-dressed tot as frontal as a doll;
Her mother smooth and round as a banister;
The oval cloudlet in the mute blue sky. . . .
Lift time's eyelid over eternity's eye.

FROM "A SUMMER SEQUENCE"

Bird and hill. The eternal roll of the skyline displaces them.
. . . And what time will outwit with weather
Makes nothing weary with green, being both envious and rife
      with matter,
Matter being treed and winged, and leafed and feathered to the
      hem.
How are they merely trivial before love — all these flowers on one
      ultra stem;
How are they, being various and sanguine-sunned and isolate
      together,
Not caring whether wind break them, whether storm mould them
      to tatter?
What makes them chirp or breathe recklessly, jewel by jewel of a
      diadem?
That eternal roll . . .
            Not love has such a secret and sure voice,
As couch to couch of one flower-bed to another
To teach continence and ration of wind and chance water . . .
No voluble distinction; no pride and no treetop-waving choice
Describe them; as this fraught heart with its multitudinous bother
Is described by acorn and chatter, tumultuously with love's arm
      and voice
         is describing a certain matter.

HYMN

For one proud moment
is the lid rolled back and fran-
tically the birth of springs releases
hood of the humble hour, in which
growth of the sensual face
creeps from the creamy white stalk
like wrinkles of a spring wound
in a faultless conformity up to
the head

no where, when men decide
lust is a moment for shock will this
momentless jack-in-the-box fail
of its head and its speech
or the wordless twinge of its
wire-filled arm, for
one curved moment is
the ruff supreme: the
nose provoked: the
mouth articulate with
rhetoric, and is the strained
mechanical form ousted for
the easied air the softer earth, suffusing
all the grave childwristed brain —

so, till the thing shall rust of
using too many times the fatal
button, dust or the remote will
will not detain
laugh of the opened lid, the stained
cheeks or the crested cap from

being shock of the moment:
faultlessly the well-known
secret fast on the click

HYMN TO APOLLO

I

Deep in man like a mountain and a mist for a tongue: the mouth like a movement; coiled in his cheek the snake of roses, and tooth by tooth as snug as music. Out like an airplane, his lips on the lips of horizon; and speaking. And speaking: the joyces of joy in the leafage, the cold fabulous books, the leaved mirrors and children: signs to provoke envy and wonder. The lock on the future, the lock-jaw: the past. And the drum, the hairless drum, of the body; and the haired.

II

High in man like a hurdle: the humhum. And a heart for an arm, a teat for a clock. And the seesaw: the eyeball and eyeball: the coiffure of lashes and the army of looking. The army of long looking. And sickness and flabbiness: the age of his richness adroop with magic.

III

Far in man and around him: the vest and the glove of idea. The glitter of his images. The flimsy statue of his footfall and the plit-plat of poetry: the plitplat of poetry and his bed. There is the sleep of his history, wigging (like a carpet of orchids) the full-length, fat-chinned apollo of his forehead, his soul on one knee! The beat here, the beat there — faint! faint! — of his buttocks, his beauteous buttocks. And the lace: the lace of his women.

IV

Low in man, the thigh of his fingers a pink blur: a white halo. The hand of his hips holding eternity. The wing of his waist — for he flies! — like a bursting bracelet of diamonds. The navel an un-tearing eye. The necklace on the neck of his middle broken: and a mussing of topaz, a bib of opal to be folded. And low on the ankle the lid of his socks, the ear of his instep: like a dream like a dream the sex: from wrist . . . from wrist . . .

V

The flash of sapphire from the mane: the nose like an initial: the head like a signature. Rising like an odor of ardors: weddinggown of his bride that he touches. Alas! — and her blindness' her blind-ness of pearls. She-she. With her glamor: if Cleopatra's mask and the asp of aching and asking. Else: the hem of Dior, the faith of Fath.

VI

And then: then the dailiness. (! and her blindness). There in man, like a clove of garlic, the actress. There, anywhere on man, the garter of death. Anywhere in man, the elastic of death. The nip of the church.

VII

The urr. The ruff of birds. The sceptre of green. The crown the crown of butterflies. By his collar of crime, the necktie of song fits: in his necktie, the pin of the nightmare sticks: from his nightmare, the name of love gleams like a star in the night of his "tails": and on this: the lily.

VIII

Where is man? where is man? In the width of his walking and the length of the moon? The roundness of Einstein and the V of vomit? There, there! In the nowhere of nonesuch! And on this . . . and on this (like a profile) the lily.

IX

Back of man: the cross of the spine, the box of the angel, and on the box the address of gold, and on the gold the gold: and on this, the lily.

X

Like a hat on man the size of heaven, and swerving like a wheel on the hat, the short plume of God almost to the shoulder. And trembling: and trembling on this: the purple: and on the purple:

XI

Naked on man, the identity, and the personality nude to the knees. Naked on man, the daughters, the sons with their arms up, their skin off half. Naked on man: the fullface. And the baby climbing naked to the fistful of fatherhood. Naked to the armpit, the fatherhood. And below this: the slice of the lily. On this: the whole lily.

XII

And nowhere, nowhere about him, and not in him, unsuspected: crepitant: curled: science. Science: science. The commodity light as a womb, large as a memo. The commodity: shaped like a war, handsome as peace. Featureless as a radio. And fumbling: gorgeous and normal: and on this: and straight: twined with it:

XIII

The dove for the second time flew forth to explore the world devastated by the waters. And on the dove: the heel of the lily.

TWO CHORUSES BY THE CLAIRVOYANTE

I

Ever in man's fist or on the breast hanging: the fetich, the charm,
the rib of a saint or his ashes, safe in an amulet:
The sign against evil: the horns against horns of the Devil:
The Host itself, blessed and reblessed, the wafer blessed for the
body, the wine blessed for the blood:
The Crucifix, no wider than finger, golden, waved in the face of
the Devil, only too eager to kiss it, using only lips as a weapon:
resurrecting in flesh the spirit, in spirit the flesh: a giddy round:
Doffing his mask to show the lover's mask: behind the lover's mask,
the skeleton, and behind the skeleton, the mind's wraith: and
pulsing amid all, the astral body, omnivalent, invisible . . .
Not a mask for the Void, the Nothing, but the Void only mask for
Body without limit, the Body whose matter is sin, dying in ar-
rested motion . . .
Lips on lips: roof and foundation for the tomb: tongue through
lips: digging the body's grave in the flesh's cave: darting, dart-
ing: infinitesimally rainbowed . . .
Living light in the body's black: the *long* kiss . . .

II

Woman the black: woman the movement incarnate: woman, peren-
nial maya, double-breasted illusion: the blind carriage:
Goddess of elementals: Kali, Kali the Black One: tinted with
night-tint, night-white and moon-savor:
Bare foot, bare buttock, blind in the navel, cruel as the first and
last earth-cluster: shaped vast and milky, blacker in the shade,
feet pounding on Shiva-Shava:

66

Shiva the living man, Shava the dead: Shiva the god-man, Shava
the limp god: two-faced and mirror-sexed: twins of the flux,
twined in the cosmos:

Shadow of scissors on their loins, lying with shadow of goblet full,
sharp-showing, wine-brimming, and one bare knife, too blunt in
her palm shut:

Woman, woman delivered and deliverer: trampling as the hooves
of the herd, unheeding: bearing, burying: drunk with her black-
ness: a-dance with her black juice: heels hard on Shiva's flesh,
flesh hard on Shava's thighs and her dark red tongue, lolling
harsh on the lips' loll, raw —

As the phallus long, riding the white teeth ridden: long, the point,
delicate: wetting her chin-fuzz . . .

KINGDOM OF THE ROSE

I

to him who wakes in madness
shall the dream be given
shall the pause be fostered
in the flowering of the rose
and slept in agony the fingers' aching
that has scratched the hours
upon the tree . . .
                  to him who in
the frenzy of the wish shall pause
to dream the fingered petals
shall smile to see the tell-tale hours
shall weep to see the shattered rose
shall smile shall weep to tuck
the dream behind his eyes
shall it be given to surround the hour
with roses dreamed into the mind
to build the castle of a prayer
for all the saints of love

II

let him who has begun to be
desire crawling to the steps of love
see in the dust the marking of the petal and
if he must press his lips to dust
let him arise and go away
to think into the dreamed-of now
to think upon the poisoned tree
to pause there in its shadow

68

and to think the rose gone mad with loving
and the open gate shall close upon a stop
unthought-of in the dreaming mind
shall close though all the dust remain unmarked
though it should be a long time since the feet reneged
that wished to make the rose smile
in the now

III

shall it be closed against the citadel
which he has builded in revoking that
where reigns the softly mirroring eyes
where sleeps the brain so tortured to the
waking of the startled hands where
in the perfect emptiness there lies
a quietness on the hands
unused to slaking of this sort
where grows an image in the brain
kept secret from the air whose
touch shall but disturb
the tendrils of his hair . . .

SIGHT COMPLEMENT

Embryo
of sound speeding
through my vague
sleep-willing
brain,

remorselessly
leaving on the
mind's film a half-
bewildering
stain,

I awake and gaze —
the sounds not stilling —
beyond where the player
sits to the window
pane,

and there, as numerous
as notes, and moving as
with sleep-bewildered minds,
goes snow — more marvelously
musical, now, than
rain.

IDIOT OF LOVE: ONE

first of first ravings, how the head, impelled toward,
is wheeled, white in eye glistening an opalescent sky,
the lashes rimming, straining as at some cloudwhite urging,
surfsurging the lolled member, curl askew, as in
sea circling quarried water's rim, the eyes write
idiocy of love: looped air's mingling, as a wheel
mingling, seeing the edge and drawing, as a pool's picture
inward making whirl, the eyes not agents but magnets for
those motes of surface the farflung furls of outwardeddying
waters suddenly giving spears of minute sight, receives
those mixing draughts of frantic water, the idiot sees
love's first shaking as air's natural home, thought's own loam,
and what thought from such madlaving stalks of air will
shoot, will idiot of love, love, first, as the rave
of infant squall on the plain sea is trembled for, will
the first wingwhips of bruised sea send surfacing about
idiot of love's racing for no winning, be trembled at, tracing
the nude forms it raves for, cries at and strikes toward,
eyes as arms, tongue as feet, runs toward, wish as deed
still in the sea of its mad home, raving, kiss nothing,
tonguelolling in headlolling as sea in sea hanging, beneath:
strange moving of things, air's several images will stars hang,
stars as in sea being, light as in dark moving, where
no line but the idiot's orbiting brings stars to the horizon;
this the first, first only, the idiot feels blindly the stars,
the farflung integers of space come to his home, hung on
his thighs like leeches, traces of sea things, saltgray
morningmooned vestiges against thighpink, sealoose ravings
of that curledblue home the tranquil ocean: star's tinsel
he knows, idiot of love stroking, his idiot finger poking
into the true texture, starfish or starflesh, slowly evoking
the glued finger flued among rheum of sea's spitting, from

71

that vast ocean knowing a splurge gulfing, a little spitting
from an end's ending: the idiot, held in the sea sitting
as winds or water hold one for a moment high and haughty,
his eyes hold or he holds, instantly, a thing witting,
love of love's self, flotsam taken curl between the thighs,
love of idiot's self, idiot's rave, first raving stiff
on his neck, second of raves is the rave stiffening after
the wave has ebbed leaving the hand down to its home come:
wave of no knowing coming and leaving a curve on the curve
of the idiot's home, the idiot's body, curving to its
neckcurve, its eyes, seacleaned, seeing its hands aroam:
the idiot's hands curve in as two waves meet beneath
seasurface in the trough of wave fondling wave, they fondle
a thing seeking depth, seeking width's length's dimension
in the bed of the waters: air's lovingest child itself, high
idiot, high, low, in the waters of moving moves slowly upon
idiot's own child, seeking space with the father, across thigh's
pink surprises own flakey one, flake or air, smooth
waterbody lodged in the cleft of rock seeking rock:
surprised, is agear with itself, its own home's owner of
one seabushy room, arhythmic of fingers' weave, tenant
as a flower is upon the unseen seaflower's floor, awave
with the fingers the idiot's fingers as a wave is aweave
with itself unseen upon the sea's bushlike floor: the idiot's
finding is itself's own supple: a wave wideeyed seeing a
wave, seeing itself's own eyes, the idiot's keeping
keeps itself undulant between seeing and being, the fingers
finding for their own and only moving move upon undulance,
kept as a wave is kept by a wave, seafound by the idiot's
own eyes, round as a waveback for a waveback to wave on:
the idiot's sheerlolling member for his love to love on.

72

IDIOT OF LOVE: TWO

wherever, tired, the idiot's feet roam, tired of it the
poking into sea's choice the wave loved back and loved on,
the wave running lovelorn, the stiff fingers unstiffening
the stiffening unstiffening and blank noons and blanker
afternoons, he finds night; night found, he is the idiot
of love unloved of the sundry waves, forking their tongues
upon loved wave's back, night found like a darkness in moving:
a wave clear and static showing the mooned member and
that alone like a bone on the mooned beach: noon for a
moment and before afternoon, night, when the tongues of
the waves mumble; his love is a tongue in the tongues
of seas in the sea, his own tongue moving in his hollow
mouth a sea in a sea and a hand and a wave: these are the
curled fragments flowing among sight of two eyes, before
the forehead flake their furlment as waves (his heart beats
a wave) fight to be waves in their own home the ocean, seek,
lolling and loving, the wave into wave of it, tongue into tongue
of it, and all, ocean; all ocean, idiot sees, and his tongue
lingering (once on his lips lingers there) lolling would live
in the ocean, a wave among waves, one wave and that ocean, one
love and that loving his own wave, his tongue's motion:
idiot of love waving his tongue, letting it, lolling, wave
its tip as a wave will tip and then lip to a wave, leers,
and the loose wave, his tongue, let loose from its loose bed
the ocean of his smirking mouth, moves upon darkness, the
dark wave of his smirking tongue loosens upon light its lymph
turning dark like a smirking wave rewaving to the ocean;
idiot laying his tongue along sand, is stung; along sand is nothing
nothing but that crave running and running lets loose
little loving for loving's end and that joy, joy for
ocean of ocean's deep rounding and each wave a tongue letting
love upon wave's back letting love loose its freeloose fists

for fun's back, back and front for love's luck, a lucky ocean
with a love of tongues and idiot's love slips backward
backward and outward and under and strikes
the idiot's image, arrived while the idiot lolled
in his own home his body and no ocean, and ocean and the
tongue lolling outward, idiot lies imageward, along the sand
reaches his hand, outward and imageward, ocean's child, ocean's
own child of one love manifest in all tongues circling
of one loved ocean, and image bobbing and fobbing, left on
land, the idiot thinks, by a sparing ocean (now it is
the idiot's notion, not ocean's), and let loose on the whole
a furled wave of a foreign ocean the tongue of the idiot
rings around round a roomy rheum, racing to the ocean, to
the ocean of colliding lilty loves, a loomed back and that
love, a back a front a front a back and up and over and
all ocean: a first foaming between idiot's tongue and loved
ocean's furl before foreign but now foaming, first frees
two idiots crushed into the ocean whose highward
foaming to a star's sickly shining, sends to that lastward
rimming of round earth's round ocean's spent running a
last loving: a curved last tiptonguing of love's moon,
slimmer to fuller, covered by ocean and ocean's loving:
lying lost moon but idiot's harbor; dream, idiot, in a dream
cave lipped by an everlipping close wave; dream, idiot, idiot
of love, your last wave into the other cave, your own cave is
dreamed and dreamed, loved; and loved, lipped by an idiot with
a lastcoming, a still to furl foaming, an other, wave.

ELEGY FOR MY MOTHER

The space is blank. But only for a moment in this
    Nervous quantity that is God's wink:
She returns like an hour on the clock, maturing
    As time matures, without ceasing
Even in the blackest night
      Or the whitest day,
From either of which the startled eye must shrink.

As the phenomenon of joy, that blossoms evenly
    On whatever bush or pile one pick,
However unseen till now, at once full-blown
    And young, all in one dress, and brilliant:
Her being obtrudes
      And pulsates
As everything else that is quick. . . .

So quick that, like a comet falling in my forehead,
    She in her girlhood flames and burns out,
Despite the languors and the questions, the delirious
    Dances, the slow swim of society through all
Her blue veins; the courtship; the
      Marriage, and finally,
Like a serpent poised on her mound of beauty and pride: Doubt.

There were many soft and sheltering nights when she lay asleep
    Dreaming, dreaming, dreaming, dreaming —
To awake unto the beautiful ambiguous fulfillment
    In the full brightness of the star, after all the twinklings,
And place together as in marriage
      The salty silhouettes
Of Doing with the milky somnambules of Seeming.

Are the gloom and the grief not mere history
    Already secretly folded in her form,
For which her name's a glisten both sad and glad?
    Deep in her depths and dark,
An ancient personal heart —
      A plastic of tears —
Beat of which she was the sculptured storm.

. . . Yet not downcast; no, as you see by the shining
    Blue of her open lucid eyes
As still, in the endless space of duration, she
    Faces, and communicates, all:
The figuration of a woman,
      A wife and
A mother . . . Is it she, indeed, who cries?

Is it she, in this whitehot flash of my memory,
    Who bows in the vessel of self,
Burned alive in her love all night, a ghost
    In the colors of morning? — Ah, this
Only lengthened her, this
      Nude poetry of love
That wept so much when she would seclude herself.

Before this began, I have wept; as she did, before
    The sudden insinuation of death
Entered the flesh of her petal of living, and
    The past became a flower in the bunch I gave.
But we have ceased to weep
      Even though, as the poem
Breathes, we both lie and weep in the same breath.

And I shall weep; and weep! And she will, repeating
    The deathless desire to know happiness
That stretches past all of us into the future,
    And if I am broken the most
For not having counted
            Her tears — well,
It is one empty gesture, among many, the less.

This is the full, the brimming sweetest gesture
    Of her dead material symmetry:
Now when the paper does not complain, or resist,
    At the heavy burden of joy I
Thrust suddenly, madly
            On its surface . . .
So love fell on her. And she let it be.

Oh, what dreadful impatience, oh! man, who has
    Love and death in the same embrace —
Prisoned in that private scream whose obscene terror
    Kisses the mouth that made it,
And coos like a baby
            On its mother's breast
And turns up its beautiful face!

Nothing frightened her except the commonest things.
    How can I suppose, even now —
In those moments, dark and insinuating, when
    She lay all alone
But recently — that she
            Was afraid?
I do not. Not after this. No. Certainly not now.

For those dark, and dark-voiced, and strange-shaped
    Forces that had bent me away
From her image so that her body was distant — once
    I had dropped from her, grown
Full to my present stature —
        Those forces,
In every tremor and accent, return today.

They hold me as though they were my backbone,
    And mould me as though they were my life.
Only last night, I stood before her in that transparence
    Belonging uniquely to a son,
And she looked at me with
        Love then, and
Love, a phantom, stood by me like a wife.

Did I say, she saw me? She never understood my
    Poetry, save only through the medium of tears
That blur, but in their opalescent clarity
    She read the curving hieroglyph
Of all my fluid life,
        Even as, in her womb,
I was a book whose hero mistily appears.

The miracle of words: ambiguity resplendent!
    One act in their grammar, having been, is yet,
And never ends . . . My heart in this rhythm shakes:
    The verse is a delicious dancing quiver
That into its muscles takes
        This single lymphatic
Surge, this dripping drama of which I am the net . . .

And nothing was, and nothing might have been, to
     Change her, who was always true;
Even the truth . . . not even Truth, the octopus
     That helps us build our cities, could disturb
Her tense love in its ideal lake,
        Whose surface at last
She breaks, like Venus from the liquid blue.

Oh, what a darling! And anyway, all the clustering
     Things that we call mind, and that
Are (hers and mine and his) our single habitation,
     Steadily denude her of mere myths —
Even the basic one — bringing
        Her forth again
As singularly charming and transient as an Easter hat.

And the more I write, the more I am sure, oh, sure
     That now too she secretly builds
The movement that is me, forming in all its elegy,
     A beauty that shall be, a lyric happiness
That clutches me when the image
        Appears that is she:
Full of the volatile fantasies with which I am filled.

Did she go? Which way did she go? Where, O God, shall I look?
     Not within the Absolute, which does not exist,
But everywhere at once! And in space, where all
     Things are — every mother, every Atlantis — fixed,
She is upon my lens
        The immutable
Cinema of grief and joy of which I am the gist.

When I move, she moves; so it was, so it will be. Even
      This is, among all the interminable rest,
The thing to be: the boring happiness, the festering cupid,
      The image surprised in a sudden, casual mirror
That turns out to be
            The only reality . . .
I am dizzy. Which, darling, is the baby? which, the breast?

HIS ELEGY

I shall be calm about us, about the terrific,
    Finger-pointing
Exclusion under the tolerant, smiling mask
Of society. Yes, others are calm, too, I know,
    But it is hard

For a man to make a girl of his ego, it is
    Difficult —
So much so! — to begin over again even the
Simple work of nature, twisting the clay for
    The cruel, complex

Sake of beauty, and facing mother or sister or
    Wife, not too
Agreeable or understanding, or too lenient
About it all, showing them themselves in another
    Skin, another form,

Another happiness. Some little boys are very
    Angels of etiquette,
Mocking their sisters, putting them to shame
Not out of malice, but envying the curls, and the
    Face of the female.

Verily, there are others, famous, of similar
    Character,
Who shape their manhood vilely, not for deity's
Sake, or darling's, merely to dictate unceasingly,
    To feel nothing

But hot inhumanity: Aphrodite who withheld.
    However, rape,

Whether real or abstract, leads to nothing
Save perhaps in a poem, perhaps in pretenses
    Of the gentle poet.

From birth, we are slaves eager to rear such
    A pyramid
Of fictitious flesh that no infant or ancient
(Both old in looking) may derive from the look
    Or the gesture

Any history for the book, as so secretly
    Our backs turn
To the truth! And with our false, thousand-eyed
Flesh helpless toward love of the lie, we then
    Make love to the lie.

Even though we poets may grow sick at thinking
    Of the torture
Common to all the genders, and then bundled
In that divine ague go home, absolutely sure
    Of Narcissus,

So fluid and flashing our world of beauty,
    We are certain . . .
Waiting for us deep in the mirror (all women
Over his face making a mask) is Narcissus,
    Criminal,

Weeping hysteria at our optimism, his male voice
    In flat prose
Saying, "You are guilty." I have answered, "How

Can we not be — famous for our feelings — having
    Seen another

Version of you, bewildered Hermaphroditus?
    Having seen in the fit
The fairy in the midst of the gay dancers,
Daring to be the gayest, the guilt seeming,
    For Cinderella,

Too much; so we preferred it. We prefer our
    Pumpkin and
Cinders to the adorable slipper of glass, that
Which at the highest peril, madness or jail,
    We would get into."

The pale and melancholy prince of guilt is
    Somewhere,
Somewhere the Hamlet of our sexuality in his
Elsinore of women. Meanwhile, we are in danger
    Of being snobs,

We who dictate to nature her most precious
    Example
Of play. Each tremendous, happy, masculine
Morning, we arise naked to the sun of that
    Paradox;

The whole world, since we are male, seeming
    Passive before
Us, and we know the abominable flattery
Of showing in the light our mother's possession
    In the black

Bedroom. How surely we were hers! Indeed, the
World was
Conquered by half of us while the other half
Waited, lying awake; or, as half lies awake in
Us now, we

Sleep on our backs, or as half sleeps if, on
Our bellies,
We conceal, or if we love: kneeling without prayer.
Oh certainly we're forgiven, else even the
Several wits of

Our rich arts could not save us from suicide.
Death hovers
Impersonally over us, and we meditate, often,
How clean and holy and unworshipable is
The killed soldier,

Far beyond our reach: and how the dead's live woman
Often thrills to
Some delightful, induplicable, dear pang of
Experience from which we are fabulously,
Fairly, excluded.

Even as others we are bored, bored horribly
With great life, soon
Soon to vanish . . . What is there to do but be
Sexual or revolutionary; make money; enjoy, over
Again, the female?

The conversation flags, and insidious, heartbroken
Socrates,

Whose pricelessly beautiful gymnasium
We inherit inside us, falls expressionless.
    Like a muscle,

The soul glistens, and hurdles; the hemlock's
    Husband
Continues silent. He will never speak again.
Something dreadful has happened. Melancholy
    Overwhelms us.

THE GRANITE BUTTERFLY

to C. Bl.
and for Philip Lamantia

chrysalis of cellophane
  through which time flows
silhouette of the expanding universe
  torn, untorn
by space's rush:
  the granite butterfly

FIRST CANTO

Birth of Art

THE mother, first in the birth pangs
Blinded with being
Crushing her lashes together
                shutting out
All but the in

And

In her: the poet
Sharing her blindness, her agony, her
Being . . .

Second:

The poet, blinded with being
First blinded, and then seeing:
But blind
            Listening
To the black music

            And then . . .
Voice: "The poet . . . "

            And then . . .
Voice: "The poet, what does he make? . . . "

And:

Out before I knew it:

Music!

Voice, mine, in the darkness
Rising from the white darkness
Voice: "What does he make?"

            A flower
Of everything a flower, only one,
Even as the world Narcissus makes
Of its image a single man, as a man
Narcissus makes of his image
A single world, a flower, no more than . . .
Twined of life, that texture, yet not
At all it, not at all life:

            but

Music from the throat, hissing like water
Water's mouth sculptured, nothing as it is

            Even the sex
            Nothing as it is
            The two sexes

Opposite, arranged for cohabiting, all one cloud
Still, one, all in the mind, one wave
Crested with hair: now fall, for it must fall,
Be done . . .
            Now the verse is a wave,
Space the beach
            On which I lay my tongue

Voice: "Out of the cloud, sound of
The piano, out of the piano . . . "
                    The image

Listen to the separate footsteps, now
Of the unseen image in its living phases
At it strains toward death the rigid flower
But never of stone, no, nothing more eternal
                    actually than
Flesh, slipping from the fingers to the keys
                    of the piano
Naively making music, unity of time, of space
Breeding into the air, bisexually, succinct
Cloud of music, heavy as the head on the body

           No heavier

Voice: "I interrupt . . . "

                    A little heavier? . . .

                    Stasis

                    INTERLUDE OF THE BLOOD

The voice no more
The whimsy of the pulse
The syllable manifest
Life falling apart
The need to go on

The heart beating anyway
Clogged music of digestion
The terrible wait
The intimations of terror
                at the roots of the hair
The intimations of terror
Why? Desire to tell everything
The sleepless watcher
                at the shoulder
The mover of the typewriter
The Voice Incarnate
Taking its shape from the flux
Taking its shape from this
                taking it from that
The rememberer
                Looking back at life
Like an enlarging tunnel
A ceaseless, nervous spiral
An eternal perspective
A rigid whirlpool:
                On its sides
Everything visible
Everything in its attitude
                Yet turning
                Because all turns:
Widening out from a beginning
As the voice widens out
As the voice emits the past
                The poet, blinded with being
Emits the past, standing in his spot
Producing his voice and all voices
From his being, his loving diaphragm

Standing, the singer:
         His lips manufacturing
The navel cord of his memory
That unbroken thing
         Till the poem breaks it

That unbroken thing, moving behind his eyes
Sound converted into image, image
Into writing, writing into vision
         Wherefore? Wherefore?

         And the voice of Shakespeare

Art thou . . . be unashamed and speak it again . . .

         "Romeo" ex-

Clamation mark the profound silence as at the end
   of a symphony the unarticulated line too often
   confused with prose but prose only a more
   mechanical formula onomatopoeia of the abstract
   Give in again: nothing
   Is more defenseless than the poet
   Faced by the firing squad of his im-
   Pulses, that do not fire parenthesis

SECOND CANTO

The Name

FROM this name take off, this platform of love

```
            XXXXXXX  XXXXXXXXX
```

Secret name of the father
        Name of another
Whole mask of the father
        In another whole being
So he be not hated
        but loved

        Breaths of being, mould!

        Not abbreviation
Nor all the sleepy grammars of this earth
Shall comma me to such deep drowse that I
Know not the sounded speech, the waking word

MORNING

As, in the subway, things go back
To their beginnings, the mind
Escaping from the sound, the seated crowd,
Going back to an old love, thrown upon its
Back, only to rise up in the poem,

Now all irrelevant sounding speech
Seems silence, all inner silence
A trembling obelisk, eternal sound
Speaking aloud in subway ad, symbol
Of motive, articulation of method,
Center of interest, trend trend
Cutting path through ancient space
Which has always been here
And always will be
               It is only Time that moves
Like a blossoming ghost
          In this Various Setting

NOON AND

So on: who in 1916 was young
       who in 1918 was older
       who in 1923 was still older
             in 1928. . . .

The hero

    From this name . . .

This madness this possession this platform
This danger this precipice this sex
This instant this rhythm this meaning
This typewriter this will but not this being

95

Only from me
This being

I am only the recorder of the hero
I am only the lover of the . . .

NIGHT?

No.   Each wrinkle of inspiration
       Each woman who could have been his
       Especially my mother
       Hiatus
       Each one is a prison
       Who could have been mine
       That I dare play
       At being free
       Who was in a way!
       Tumultuous:
       A beautiful line
       That I dare play
       In this way
       Makes an earth of sound
       Makes a beginning of
       A story that must be told
       How marvellous the sense
       Of freedom as I grow old
       (Here the deliberate rhyme!)
       In this cage, Age, the dull thud
       Of stupid rhyme the wise eyes
       Of lies
            down and goes to sleep

96

Anything, anything

         to make an end

So as to begin

THIRD CANTO

Boredom

BOREDOM
A PLAY

SCENE: Complicated perspective. Off a newly laid road in the mountains, now convenient for two-car traffic, a narrow road branches off at right angles and climbs between heavy woods, in an up-and-down, this way and that, fashion to a point where, at a sharp turn of the way to the right, the woods to the left suddenly cease, turning into a large gradually descending field of grass, weeds, and blackberry bushes, and revealing, at the terminus of the broad field, a neat, white-painted house. But dwarfing the house, like a backdrop that overwhelms the elements of the middle and fore grounds, a superb vista extends for hundreds of miles into a literally blue distance — this effect being emphasized by the fact that one regards the house from a prominence which is evidently only the beginning of a valley over which the house itself sits. The nearer distance behind the house, with its tiny houses and minute roads over which toy vehicles move, is brilliant with the mottling of early autumn, which, at this moment approaching sunset, seems to reflect the colors of the sky. In the farthest, mauve-blue distance, to which the eyes are drawn as by a magnet, the mountains have the phantasmal substance of the mountains in Chinese paintings, seeming to drift upon air, and possessing the soft outlines of clouds. The road toward the house follows the edge of the field for a space, the woods continuing on the right, then winds to the left through the field, and after a slight right turn, brings you up before the crude, white-painted wooden fence with its wide "cow-gate," separating the lawn before the house from the road. But before the gate is swung open to admit you, you have had an opportunity to appraise the house, its simple grounds, and the structure that forms

98

the left hand boundary to the lawn: a red-painted barn that serves for a garage. The house itself is of the Colonial type, with big chimney and slanting gables, toylike in comparison with the immense branching tree that over-spreads almost the entire lawn to the right, but actually commodious inside. To the right of the house, halfway between it and the fence, are twin crabapple trees, now laden with their fruit like two girls with bangles and ribbons in their tresses; between them a bright-striped hammock is strung. Imbedded stones pave your way to the vine-draped, simple front-door, but before entering, you are aware of the elaborate grape arbor at the left end of the house, sheltering the entrance to the kitchen.

ACT ONE

HE: Come here.
SHE: (Invisible) Why?
HE: Come here.
SHE: In a minute.
HE: Can't wait.
SHE: (Appearing) What is it?
HE: Guess.
SHE: Oh, that. Oh, that.
HE: Never know.
SHE: Might have known.

CURTAIN

HE: Name of God.
SHE: What's the matter?
HE: Where's breakfast?
SHE: Come and get it.
HE: Trying to fool me.
SHE: Aren't you fooled?
HE: Never around you.
SHE: What's wrong with me?
HE: Nothing.
SHE: Something.
HE: Don't say it, let me guess.
SHE: Guess.
HE: No.
SHE: Never mind.
HE: Feeling bad?
SHE: Not . . . especially.
HE: Last night . . . ?
SHE: Oh, not that.
HE: Never that, huh?
SHE: Maybe! (A brief pause.) Oh, God, it's too wonderful.

(They kiss.)

(Enter the Poet before the curtain.)

POET: I was gracious enough to wait till the end of the Second
    Act. I am not restrained by nature; nevertheless, restraint
    is one of my métiers. I have all the time in the world in
    which to tell anything. Hence my peculiar impatience. My
    walking in at odd moments. And my walking out at odder

ones. But in the end, it's all the same. I'm forgiven. If not beforehand, then afterwards. I fear nothing but silence, although silence itself is one of my subtler instruments. I have meant this little play — as is obvious, I am the author — to be extremely commonplace. Yet full of life, redolent with the flavor of living, something of the people's speech. Just so nothing would go wrong. So there wouldn't be any misunderstanding between me and my audience as to whom or what I meant, or that sex of a very ordinary, lustful kind is meant. Perhaps you think this speech of mine is vulgar. Maybe it is. But lay it down to my excessive conscience, my sense of scruple, and my fear. I tend not to fear silence because silence is when I recuperate for further speech. In a sense, this negatively therapeutic process is true of everyone. But to me — I am a poet — speech is a wound. Contrary to a certain popular notion that I personally am inclined to be verbose, I say only what is absolutely necessary, for it pains me a great deal to say anything. You see, I may not say it properly. I may not say exactly what is in my head. Even now, as I make these explanatory remarks, I am afraid that I may be going amiss, that I may not be saying exactly what is in my head. But the main thing with artists is that something be in the head, something tremendously difficult to exhume, like a mummy in the heart of a pyramid. At first, I did not mean to say anything figurative in this prose speech, but you see, I have. And it has a great deal to do with the scheme of the poem. Wait, and see. One of my traits, I say without shame (and without shame simply because it must be said), is that I am perverse. I am perverse enough to believe in the twentieth-century revelation (or did it happen before?) that whatever a person thinks should be expressed in a convenient and

(Iris in on play)

HE: This is life.

SHE: It's paradise.

HE: Never want to see the inside of a studio again, or the face of
    a camera.

SHE: Love me?

HE: (Says nothing)

SHE: Love me?

HE: I was just thinking.

SHE: What were you thinking?

HE: If this is all there is to life, but—

SHE: Don't think such things.

HE: (Finishing) — of course, it is.

SHE: Is what?

HE: Life . . .

(A negro boy walks in laden with two large paper bags full
of groceries. His eyes fix themselves on the woman and he stares
silently at her. Beautiful and terrible music bursts on the scene.
It seems as though one's heart might break. The man and woman
are like statues. The boy puts down the groceries and walks out
like a somnambule. On his forehead, the audience reads the word:
"Oedipus.")

FOURTH CANTO

Portrait

CONSCIENCE, color of night and color of day
Beautiful thing! rising
Like Venus from the waves of being
Link, link to all, leader moving
Backwards, facing forward
  Self
And environment, backward from the mirror
Narcissus moving, transfixed alike
With fear and love, moving back
To get the perspective: "What is behind me?"
  In front
Only the self-image
        But is it?
Not Perseus?
    Not the Medusa?
Not the furious mother? Between her
And the father, the son, facing away,
Holding the mirror
       daring
To look not at her,
        but he too
Seeing the father?
       Elision
Of pasts, none his, and yet all
In the widening mirror of conscience, part
His, hanging in ether, handed down
Lying in books, alive in the mucous
Atmosphere of continued being
          animal

105

Racial, terrestrial stirring
                    Insistent
With a life of their own
                    bearing down
Weighted with weight of the atmosphere
Romeo:

          stepping forth as the actor
Who never impersonated him:

                    flawless
Specific

          Point of the nose
Long, classic, virile, out
From the face
                    Nostrils pyramidal
Flatulent, openings almost
Level with the bottom
                    line
Of the nose in profile
          Agony of
Identification, it was He
Not the father, yet this too
Somewhat applies — No! No!
Agony of itness, stranger
To the house, not even a visitor
Not even acknowledgement — unknown
Save as an image shining out
Of the cinema heaven, dropped like a day

From eternal time, a star swimming
        upright
As he did in the current in that movie

       Relatively
Short upper lip
Primness of lip forms
Slightly effeminate
             Hair, too,
Unmasculinely long; wavy, black, a
Trifle manelike
          and the Cheeks
Fat for the slender forehead; sweeping
Classical curves rounding up away
           from the neck
Neck slight and short for length
         of the jaw
The chin dipping in a double rondure
Curving back to the knob in front unsplit
With dimple, pointed yet not so
Pointed
      as the Nose
          cheeks
Aging full enough to mould
The lines accenting the sensual,
Pointed pouches on either side
         of the painted mouth
Made up, of course, for the camera: tightened
         expression, under lip
a trifle protrusive, of a
brittle harshness, dandyish pride:

Below:
Stance of a lounging horse on hind legs,
Accent of belly —

                    Curtain

"Rape in the Jungle" title never given:
                    Movie
Never done: Lugubrious verse: Killed verse

Death Life Love Beauty Eternity Soul God
Phallus of the Thesaurus
                    "The delicacy
Of the point above in contrast
With the grossness of the point"
                    the poet to his friend
                    "below"

                    :above
Some ineffable sniff
Some disorientation
Some complicated patina
As though the Maker had
Been preoccupied with
Some ontological problem
Making the nose
                    complete in itself
Unrelated
          Yet
it is symbol for, is it not?

(above man, below animal)

and all handsomeness
elegance, suavity
as at extremities of a
racehorse

INTERIM

Where is our home, in one place?
but gross, gross
As the pendulous world, sick
Medusa, asleep at the hips of Narcissus
Knife only for making children

above:
the flabby chest
narrowness of the shoulders
below: subtle
Fatness of haunch
below:
subtle fatness of haunch
— the belly opulent, and irresistible
— and something else irresistible
and the throat: overfull, soft
starting close to the base of the neck:
another curve, irresistible

legs, slender

ankles: too thin

FIFTH CANTO

Metamorphosis

To take from the air
Thought's inevitable feature
                Too much
Concerned with the technique of knowing
Too little with the technique of being
                Too much
For the fluid stream of red that winds
Infinitely invisible on blind horizons
                in that permanent
Shadow, broken into only by violence, the
Body: too much for it, narcissistic
Emblem, unwilled hub of the universe, extending
Its senses automatically into space
                Solid or ethereal distances
Verifiable unit
                from the cradle outward
                forward
Verifiable complex
                from the cradle inward
                backward
Growing two ways, two methods
At once, complicated as number
Proceeding at once to the father
                and the past
Yet growing in the shade of the father
                who is tree who is sun
Proceeding
                knowing Height is Future
                "the Past" throwing its shadow
Before, "putting its hand" on the arm

110

Of the future in restraint or urging
                    Going back to the mother
After roaming, back to safety
                    of the vertical present
Where there is curling and roundness
                    the womb posture
Growing lengthier supine, in sleep
                    breeding the priapus
                    first symbol of the
                    vertical man
Who outsteps the father

                    . . . Look
at the pyramid: Man supine
its base: feet toward you, head away:
at the top, tip of the penis
that holds it up: apex of the pyramid
Abstract tent of sleep, passive
                    geometric
                    desire —
tip it backward for loving . . .
no need to: it is built
          to be seen from the base:
lover in the dust at its feet . . .

Who insteps the self, roving
Around the interior of the body
The mind like a hunter, idle
In a forest of No Animals, in
The forest virgin of all but memory
Beginning with consciousness:
                    And the mind

Growing like a tumor, filled with
Bookprint, conceptions of other beings
                    WHERE ARE THEY?
Those personalities who lived, loved in a play
Died there only to live in memory
To achieve deity equivalent to charm?
                    Convertible
In an instant from anything:
Chicks from the egg of boredom
Who feeds them at evening?
                    where do their calories come from?
They, who are always the same age,
Weight, height: unvarying in the timeless
Vault of Heaven, name of vaguely arched space?
Called from the page like a name from memory
Ready, like a servant, at beckon
They, slaves to the accidents of attention:
Buried in books as in loam:
Flowering in an instant, Narcissus of
                    non-mirrors, waiting
For strangers to recognize them:
Blinded by their own being
                    as a fruit by its sheath
Their names printed on them like beggars
Awaiting donation of eyes . . .
                    At last in their graves,
Merely as a convention, playing possum
                    They, a supine
Wink in the darkness
Ready to spring from the several wombs
                    whence they came again

Their life
                    undiminished by distance
Snug, in the child who plays with them
                              as paper dolls,
As circles of the tree bole in the body
                         of the tree
Layer on layer,
                    excrement too their divinity
Tender on the tongue
                    their trembling tissue
This is it: the poetic alchemy: the single
                    fluid substance, redolent
                    of all
Yet of nothing
                    in particular

(Exhaustion of voice, poise of pencil
More architecture, but the architecture
Will come as the story will come, as it will:
Poet in a trance, only playing possum
Pencil a penis, children of words, white
Page: a seduced virgin claptrap but
Beautiful claptrap: ultimate objective:
                              leisure
The freedom to speak: poem a pretext)

                         Spoken
the Story whose animal life, I point, existed
And exists, snarled in tenses as in a net:
                         animal
Becoming snarled with itself, unwilling
To assume again the womb posture, trussed

113

In a second womb: ignominious death
Death by the enemy, the lurking assassin
Death by the poet, the magic assassin
Charming the story itself and the content
                    of the story
Marrying the form to the content, whose
                    child he is
The part of the story which is the mother
                    is the content
The part of the story which is the father
                    is the form
He marries them in the poem, he the
                    Matchmaker
Poem the match made, over again
                    Jealous
Of the content that is the mother
                    jealous
Of the content that is the father . . .
                    confusion
Then in intensity of his jealousy

Story the child of the parents?
Their story, beyond his reach?
                    Only repetition?
No. Form: the active element
                    But suppose
The content is masculine, the
                    mother is
Masculine-minded,
                    hesitating Oedipus?
Oedipus in the dark, black Oedipus
                    Intruder: then

Some of the form is in the content
                    So some of the content
Must be in the form. Love of Jocasta
Tempered with pity of the
                    Displaced: not Father
                    but Masculinity:
Quality of manhood, so still hatred
                    Still masculine
Desire of the son for the mother, but
                    Hatred (tempered
By pity) for the father, the feminine,
                    creating kindness
In Killing: nothing so like kindness in
Killing as killing
                    by Sex: logic
                    of metamorphosis:
Vagina of the story, willing to be born
as a child wills to be born: willing
                    not to be born as
as a child wills not be born: line
                    limited
by the edge of the paper: story
                    unlimited

SIXTH CANTO

Black Oedipus

I LIFT the curtain of Black Oedipus himself
To show you an historic act:
                    the Day

Black Oedipus (conscience) said
            "Whah sh'l Ah put these?"
                    insolent
But they paid no attention to him, till —
One day — he surprised them as they lay nude
Together, upstairs in bed, surprised them
                    As . . .

A lie is, in essence, nothing but
                    rape, rape of the truth
"But you always tell the truth . . . "
It's simple I said I keep out of situations
            where I have to lie:

Only the commonsense notion of a lie
Only the uncreative conception of a lie
            : the defensive lie
Lying your way out
Laying it with sawdust bricks
In the end: escape by a hair's-breadth
Else the simple falsehood

            the fraudulent front
Thus fantasy by builders of the past
            who have nothing to hide in it
            but their own arrested development

116

Still: the defensive lie
Defending self-vacuity
The stunted personality
The shell-like soul
      Within: void
      Within: void or
The aim of the imposter
But at least his lie creates
A well-knit front, the
      whole costume, tailored
      and pressed

The virtuous principle of the lie is its
      contradiction of the truth
And it derives its importance from the
      importance of the truth
Building the flesh up to the soul's letdown.

The secret of the effectiveness of art is the
      accuracy and magnitude of its lie, raping
      the truth in the middle, the place
      it should be raped
And the largest truth

      from this a dialectic

"Get the hell outa here, you . . . . . . "

Rise up of white man naked from bed
Standing of black man clothed in the door
Outcry of white woman:
      Unmoving

Oedipus, less tall by a head, slighter
In build but illumined, full as a night-
        sky of static encirclement
"Why, you . . . " redrush of anger to white man
         suffusion of honor to fingertips
         tingle of spine: vague fear as of
Fate, yet stepping toward, fists clenched
         A profile of outrage
All decency, law, honor, and race on his side
         Oedipus
Innocent, slight as a boy, blind as a curtain
         yet Eye Incarnate
Eye into an arm, arm into Destiny
         Destiny into Doing

They grapple, rustle
Of struggle and woman respiring
         faint, too scared to move, woman
Pure in this moment, absolute as symbol
         of possession, having only
To be, to be wonderful, yet as an individual
         Now in love
Mortally concerned for her love yet unable
         To move
Unable to move yet able to breathe to exult
         To register
All that is happening, as though it happened
         Within her
As though she had willed it, melting —
         Her body
On the bedsheet, pink in the white room, flushed
         in her ecstasy

Her eyes closed like a doll's, her ears open like a doll's
Hearing the struggle in the hall, then sound of
                    falling, "They have
Fallen down the steps"

                    Oh, unable
To move, even to find out what kind of fate
Today has for her, simply a woman: enough
                    Her hair limp as a
                    lifeless hand, her hand
Unlimp as a waving tress: both hers, she
                    alone, the sounds
Of destiny retreating, she triumphant . . .
                    the Open City

                    Title: "Through the
V of a butterfly's wings," flicker of
Fate, image of white form running, blood
                    from his lip, limpingly, across
The lawn to the gate, pursued
His eyes wild, by the black
                    one, shirt half off: the white
in the sunshine (all nature a witness, staring
                    at the exotic accident) stumbled on
the rut in the road: "crubble" of stones: "thnud"
                    of knee: "snut" of palm:
                    "crut" of elbow
Rolled over on his back across the rut
                    Eyes crushing
Their lashes to blot out the black in blackness
                    Letting his arms relax
                    No help now, the world

119

Far away, unconcerned, the grocery wagon
                     standing there, he knew,
By the garage, full of boxes, driver's
                     seat empty, waiting . . .

                     Fear for life
Growing like a stake in his heart, strength
Gone, not only humiliation, horror, now, maybe
                     death, too, love no
More? Some defense in the gauzy air?
None? Nothing? No, not
Nothing — instinctively, like
                     the spontaneous reflex of the nervous
                     system to a mortal blow,
                     drawing his knees up
Toward the chin, sloughing in an instant
                     adulthood
And even sex — fearful (Narcissus) of blemishing . . .
                     his motion coincident
With flicker of butterfly's wings through
                     which like a window: exact angle:
Stop the film and see for yourself:
                     Then go on
Start it, smashing of butterfly, defense's chimera,
                     Time's guardian angel, by onrush of
Laughing Oedipus, dark as inside of the lid
                     shining black in the day, naked as space
Downrush, ironic grin of the savage mask, white teeth,
                     for none but green-eyed summer
To see —
                     inrush!

                     120

Groan from the seat of all toppling worlds
            nudged from their orbits

        and inrush . . .

And . . .
         the whole white body seeming to
Heave on the other's polarity, like a
           discontented sleeper, or a ship
             settling in the trough
               of some great wave . . .

         in the dining salon
a basket of fruit by the surge of the sea
           tipped backwards
from the gaze, dumped out on the table
           its pendant peace
Spoiled, its gravity Shaken
           its Contents reassorted . . .

SEVENTH CANTO

Slow As

SLOW as the first long look of love
Slow as the last look
Slow as the music of a sigh
Slow as the moment after goodbye
Slow as the meaning of a dream
Slow, slow as the dream is quick
Slow as the puzzled gaze of the sick
Slow as the opposite of vertigo
Slow as the heart when time is short
Slow as flowers growing
Slow as the moon's dance
Slow as the young thinking
Slow as the eyes opening with surfeit of sleep
Slow as the pensive drinking

Slow as the whole head turning from sight of the truth
Slow as the logic of Ruth
Slow as a deadly aim
Slow as a ride for pleasure's sake
Slow as the tongue of terror
Slow as the bridal march
Slow as a deliberate error
Slow as a grief-striken butterfly
Slow as the day you die

Slow as a never-before-heard sound
Slow as your name on the lips of another
Slow as a forgiving mother
Slow as the fall from grace
Slow as a smile fighting for life on a face

Slow as birth
But not as slow as death
Slow as a king's condescension
Slow as a saint's ascension
Slow as Freud's triumph over his opponents
Slow as the soul's breathing
Slow as the World Revolution
Slow as a knife's sheathing

And slow as rhyme
Slow as endless time
Slow as a walk around a dime
And slow as every clock
Slow as a bullet leaving the brain
Slow as a spreading stain
Slow as an inch of rain
Slow as a drowned man
Slow as an awkward child
Slow as the vertical words of confession
And slow as Oscar Wilde

Slow as the necessary
Slow as a drugged salesman
Slow as the wary
Slow as an escaping thief
Slow as a falling leaf
Slow as the one who drops the handkerchief
Slower than the one who picks it up
Slow as an almost overturned, but righted, cup
Slow as a loosening embrace
Slow as the greetings of the old
Slow as the overbold and the underwed

Slow as the one who arrives at the house of his mother once more
And slow as the wind-wafted door
Slow as the desire to end
Slow as this paradox of all slowness
Slow as things falling seen directly from below

. . . And slow as echo

Slow as the last bounce of the vanquished on the indifferent ground
Slow as the approach to the pyramid while it grows taller
Slow as a poem on death
Slow as the undulations of the snake that had its head crushed
         by the heel of Christ
Slow as the relaxing victor
Slow as emptying space
And slow as one more
"Let's have one more, dear," he said . . .
Slow as doubt, reproach, and yearning in one form
Slow as the instant of levitation high above the turmoil so

The slowness of it . . .
         as of a thing
      in the heart of a pyramid
      white, yet wrapped in the dark
      a thing as unseen and old
      as young and new as a priceless
      relic, and the fruit

That was spilled out by the tremendous force begin-
      ning somewhere with infinite
      effort along the seabottom

even this, not exhausting the
time it took to form the
motion, but no — the opposing
forces already having set up
between the stars and the earth's
axis

A trembling armistice: this only the precise
            repercussion, or one of them:
            hieroglyph, alive and visible, trans-
            forming itself as all things in
            nature do, even the invisible
            heart of a pyramid

Now the white sex having been tumbled
                        (arbitrary, arbi-
            trary the timing)
                    heels over
            head, moving like a white snake
            struck in the throat and vanquished
            amidst its nest, showing all nature
            in sunshine what habitually clung
            to the ground, sliding, the under-
            side

                        Suddenly
The pyramid disappears from around its heart
            leaving the heart there on the desert
            sands, black and white hieroglyph
            still in the same duration, itself
            complex of pyramids

Till all the desert flowers into Home:
>the green, the road, the gate, the
>lawn, the house, she upstairs
>>unconscious, or
>>conscious as a tranced
>>sibyl, her lips trembling
>>wild and stunned

The great tree spreading over the east fence
>Subtle among its leaves
>its individual leaves
>>sun-flecked

And

Outside, having come in the meantime: Egypt
>like a dropcurtain, sand and pyramid
>painted flat, and vast African distances
>>hovering in dirty blue
>>heat, below:
the Duration, the actual
>heart of the duration
>beating, warm, dimen-
>sional, simulated
sand of the painted drop
>joining as it ends, real
sand of the desert, on which
>like an island in the
midst of the verdure, strange music
has taken

Form: plastic architecture trembling in its birthsweat.
baffling blueprint outspread:
the
legs of the black, smaller shape of the
foreground outlining the
pyramid's broad base at the
bottom, tip in the heavens
legs of the white, larger shape of the
middle ground, bent at the knees
kneeling on air, marking with
each knee, base of an inverted
pyramid (nothing but sky-mirage
bee buzzing through)

Pyramid's
tip, vanishing point solid on the
ground and joining (somehow) tip
of the other upright pyramid
to make an

X

. . . . mask, mask of the abdicating king,
king playing possum to escape
death, to achieve immortality even
to the vanishing point, far realm
of the pyramid
Consider
now yourself a grain of sand (take
this one as an example) related to the
Great Pyramids of Egypt: your size is
as one grain, but for this pyramid, there

is a smaller grain, to which it is as
big, and by its com-
            Plex

Structure is analyzable into shapes and sizes
            though relatively shapeless, sizeless
                    as a grain of sand is:
            even so, sand makes the Desert, whose oedipal
            blackblue shadows rise up Alone,
                        Shadow

Of the pyramid
            tip joining tip
                    on the other side of the

World: at the bases
                Peace of joining:
                        at the tips

War . . .
            King collaborating not only with
            the narcissus poet but with neces-
            sity: if placed in a helpless
            position, faked trance after all is
            better than death, temporary
            retirement better than suicide: every day

Even in the movies,
                even the Japs
                die by their own hand rather
                than . . . then, interrupting
                duration, as it does always — as

An airplane
        the duration of the desert or
        a butterfly, duration of the summer
        — each capable of viewing from above
        what providential pyramid falls
        under their alert, alien attention

                Whatever

Simulacrum of a thing
        neither, precisely, peace nor war
                (necessary as prose
                arbitrary as poetry)
        is found whole beneath their vision

Whatever
        transparent, immaculate pyramid
        be seen — in strange
        skeletonic interpretation
                . . . even

Pneumatic
        flesh and its histories
                proving the abundant variety
                of any pyramid's heart, in-
                sistent, abandoned
        disregarding its milieu, all the
                forms of matter and their
                laws of behavior, according to
        which it occurs, because actually
                it is the nutrient, secret

dynamite of those laws, anti-climactic
because its value is always
circumstantial —

Slow as . . . .
Slow as . . . .
Slow as . . . .

the Orgasm

EIGHTH CANTO

Narcissus

STROPHE

ETERNAL Narcissus
    fixed first
        by his immobility
Counting the nights
        swinging over
Him and the revolving days
        as nothing
Seeing the stars never
        as architecture but
Always as a shower
        of stars
               Heaven
Molten, and the day
        running gold, full
Of flying fragments from the
        original disturbance, whose
        static essence he is:

Sitting, unsighing
        Anatomy, various
        unvarying Entity, the

Moonlight only an-
        other phase of
Cosmic nervousness, recurrent
        as a chill, fickle as

Fate: renewing itself con-
   stantly in the same
    stupid experi-
Ment to find finality

      the
Moonlight only the bursting
    of another ulcer
Announcing, with restless
    eternity, the origi-
Nal injury

     He, he alone
     healed wound of

The universe:

     Even the sun
Seeming to make all dance,
    being (down to the light
     in his eyes)
Only the central
    incorrigible burning
On the expiring Body of Matter
     He
The essential, watchful Organ,
     exempt
And critical, measure of Chaos
     whose darling
He is, without relatives
    or lovers, jealous

Of nothing, the most fortunate, the
                    chosen
Flower

Of course, false:
                    because he is
The statue, the pure image
                    without entrails
He having lent them
                    to the world, false:
Because myth is relative
                    in both time and space,
The trouble with myth is
                    it has had no criticism
That would have placed its
                    anatomy in time, have
Measured it in the space of
                    that time, thought of it
As functional, but how can you
                    think of as functional
Now, what was functional then?
                    So myth has always been
A lie, the moment it was uttered
                    just as, the moment it was
Uttered, it was also a truth:
                    it was a lie to test
The truth, and a truth to test the
                    lie, being ambivalent toward
Itself
                    as Narcissus is

133

Ambivalent toward
            himself, as all con-
Cepts, once they are con-
            ceived of as Natural
Contradict themselves
            Nature
Being subject to change —
            So Athens
Falsely placing Socrates in
            Nature, measured
The lie of the Platonic
            truth, placing it in
Nature, where there is change
            where Beauty is
Not an absolute idea, but
            relative, being self-
Conceiving and other-conceiving
            loving and beloved —
Subject to change in itself, and
            through that change
Changing its ideas about changing
            others, inducing them
To conform to its will, and failing:
            revising its ideas
About its will, relating itself to
            possibility and proba-
Bility, choosing between this
            type of action and that,
This function of contemplation and
            that, sometimes this
Being Art
            but so natural

No man cares to tell it
      from life . . .

The negro, after being in too much of a hurry
To rape the woman, too,
          got out of town
And everyone, apparently, got over the fright
          and the nastiness of it.

But —
      that was no end to it
As there is no end
To the idiot fascination of
Narcissus waiting for
      Image to turn into
      Flower, flower into
      Pyramid
Self to become what he sees
        Self
Only the most obvious desire,
Sure, first of all, of self-
Love, after that. . . .
      Note of the poet
      scribbled on the back
      of an
Envelope: "Love,
      cloud in the shape of a pyramid
      appearing only as reflection
      on still water of desert sand —
      only, at noon as at midnight,
      in the oasis of self, there
      at the heart of the pyramid: such

mummies as only the self has
known, such real or possible
things as make the memory
one"

Looking perfect in print

All this as nothing
              in the daily triumphing of
Desire, all this as only
The symptom of an activity
              the involuntary spasm
Convulsing the consciousness
              as it does the page, desire
In the irresistible journey
              of the eye toward
The horizon, embracing all
              it encompasses with
              flesh of
Its body: expressing
              that prime promiscuity
              lodged in the
Soul of Narcissus, naive
              investigator in
Perpetual attitude of prayer
              praying that flower appear,
Self vanish
              be
Lost,
              melt through the
Visual apertures
              in the untimed flood

Of seeing, merge with
          the
Current of
          simultaneity
Slipping through the
          eyeballs, smoothly
Without displacement
          unknown, unre-
Cognized
          as an invisible Stran-
Ger,
          complete yet
Nothing tangible, whole
Yet the
          smallest part, littler
Than
          the littlest grain of
Sand —

There, there, there:
          in the midst of everything that
          is, was, or will be, growing
like a fountain, shaped like a vase,
          an inverted
          pyramid,
              whirling:

NINTH CANTO

The Story

... "I'M darned if I can see myself in that
Russian picture, Count Alexei Escutonoff, what
A moniker, distantly related to the Czar, and with
Class, gold braids and white uniform, tight pants
Of a Hussar or are my nations mixed, honey? married
But falls in love with a peasant girl on his
Wife's brother's estate, then there's an uprising
Of the peasants, things like that used to happen
In Russia, and the Count's love affair with the
Beautiful peasant is at its height, and it's
Been discovered by his wife —

              that's you, my dear, unless
You mind very much my being unfaithful to
You, do you?

              — and their life is about to be
Ruined, or something, anyway, this rebellion thing —
I wonder if he has a mustache, well I'm not going
To — happens and upsets the applecart, the palace
Or whatever they live is a wreck and — who d'yah
'Spose saves the day, smuggles them all
Out the back door, yes, the beautiful peasant
Girl who has a heart of gold under her Russian
Smock and can't see the handsome Count —

              Me, of course —
Lose his noble wife's love, the devotion and
Respect of his little kiddies, so —

              well, so
She sets everything right, but that's too much
Of a role for her, where do I come in?

138

                    I must
Look rather silly, hiding in the skirts — and the
Dirty skirts at that of a mere woman . . . "

"Well, I like that — "

"That's what I mean, of a mere woman, why
Can't I fight my way out? That's what I
Usually do, I do have a duel, just to show
I'm really in love with my wife, it's over her
Honor, you know, and that's the way the
Picture begins.

                    Well, what do you think? . . .

I kill the guy . . . Well?"

                    This was 1932

That night she dreamed:

                    subtle influence of mys-
                    tical emanation in the
                    omnipresence of Narcis-
                    sus or some such
                    rot, "an overture"

. . . the left wing of the mansion afire
                    . . . Liza and Rupert
in the arms of Katerina, their nurse
      the fat woman trembling beneath her silk

eyes popping out, her fury exploding, her
    fear making her tense, controlled
but shuddering at the truth of it,
                     Alexei
downstairs, her last glimpse having been
    his figure stalking to the staircase,
his back visible from the master bedroom
    where Katerina suddenly sat on the bed-end
triply collapsing with the two children
    Liza weeping, like one side of the nurse's
nature, Rupert taut, boiling like the
    other, yet sickened a little, like her,
at events to come

            Alexei's jacket
open, the gold braid parted in the center as,
    sword gleaming from the chandelier's light
at the bottom of the staircase, he
    clattered down, shouting to his soldiers
and the few serfs who had run in,

                  the cook, then,
opened the door from the sitting room
    back of the bedroom, her face red as
a beet, huge, tearing from every pore, she
    had never been in the Countess' bedroom
but now she strode in like a team of oxen,
    proud of the occasion that released her
from asking permission for the unique
    intrusion
yet not malevolent, merely flabbergasted, heaved
    by the cyclonic event upstairs, wavery

140

on her feet that went before her and pushed her
    long skirts apart like scuttling animals

        "Bitka!"
admonished the Countess in a subtle rebuke
    yet thanking the gray-haired serf
for her presence while in a flash she saw
    the new female existence like another
great baseless timber, helping in the
    catastrophe that made all tremble, so
she wished her away, sending her a silent
    glance full of deep reproach, killing
as a dagger.

      The serfs were firing — where
had the guns come from? Probably brought them
    by the revolutionists, or hidden for
weeks in preparation for this ghastly,
    accursed moment of treachery . . .
She saw them seething at the great door, faces
    so often smiled at in the past with
that melting smile that fell from the formal
    frigidity of her face not so much like
a smile as a tear, fluid, leaving her
    lovely warmth normal again, raised to
the sky that sent down its perpetual smile
    on her aristocracy, her happiness with
Alexei
    but the girl, the one
She was suspicious of because she saw the
    way she looked at Alexei one day by the

road, and had the haunting vision that they
    had some secret knowledge of each other —
she had not dared admit it even to herself,
    the suspicion they may have seen each other
in the summer fields at night, Tanya ascend-
    ing again to her pride, so unassailable
in the mansion that was hers and Alexei's . . .
        theirs?
Now, was it theirs? Now what did Alexei's
    infidelity matter, only in this
moment did she realize it, admit it was
    true. It could not be otherwise, not
with the knowledge given to women in
    love. How much she wished for time
to be turned back, to go back to Alexei's
    betrayal, so these sounds could be exiled
from her ears, shouts that seemed to grow
    louder, crashes — certainly the great door
was going. Was there no escape? She looked
    at Bitka — something was missing —
Bitka was kneeling, crossing herself before
    the Ikon in the corner of the bedroom . . .

Katerina was staring at her, mouth open.
    "Are they in the kitchen, you praying fool?"
        rasped the nurse
"Are they devouring our food, drinking our
    wine perhaps?" She was accusing.

        The Countess thought:
"This is not happening as it should, there
    ought to be some help. Where was the Czar?

How was the Empress, were they too, perhaps — "
      The thought was too terrible, her eyes
Suddenly saw Rupert, about to struggle from
      the nurse's arms, Liza's head burrowing
against one breast, the boy had hold of
      the other, clasping it and yet thrusting
it off — her children, hers and Alexei's, now to
      perish — ?

          She screamed, clear and high the sound
rose up, seeming to the astonished group to
      pierce the roof and soar off into the
night. As they all trembled, gasping, Rupert
      broke loose from Katerina and running
met Alexei at the door. At this moment, Bitka
      whose head whipped around at the Countess'
cry, fell over like a barrel, slightly in the
      direction she had turned her head, teetered
for an instant, and lay still
                her face redder than before

    "My darling!" Alexei's voice, emanating from
Alexei's body, her own, her precious husband,
her only hope, support, sun and moon of her
happiness, wild concern now in his eyes, but
looking straight at her, excluding all else
even the children, his braided cuff knocking against
Rupert's face, the boy's hand going to the spot
      as though he had been struck,

          Tanya
felt limp suddenly, desiring proof of his arms

yearning for one last rehearsal of their love in
this fiery black-framed moment, one instant
if only one, of pretense, but the smoke
suddenly came to her nostrils, invading all
her being with reality, and she stiffened
before he reached her.

"Where?" she gasped. "Where can
we go, Alexei? They are here. We are lost!"
Alexei clasped her but instinctively she
felt his warm arms cold, for they pushed against
her silky dressing gown, and it was cold — Oh,
for some icy retreat, some place even in the
cold, some hut . . . Why were they all like
statues? Surely the world out there held some
refuge, this could not be the end . . . Her eyes
went deep into Alexei's, asking straightly, no
wish coming from her heart to be deceived,
a glance such as she had never given him about
the girl ——
He closed his eyes.

"I thought you were hurt. I thought they were
here!" was his reply. It brought things
back to the time in which they were, to the tide
of villainous, maddened serfs that were
about to sweep up the staircase — oh, why had
the Emperor never allowed them more men,
more faithful soldiers, to guard them from
harm? Was he selfish, was he wicked, did
he ——?

Seeing her face so alien now, Alexei said,
　　low: "Do you wish to die before you are taken?"
But the nurse's ears heard. "We can hide in the
　　attic," she blurted, distraught. "They'll
steal first, they'll want all we have, not us.
　　Come!" She collapsed with Liza as she took
her first step, tripping and sending the child
　　pellmell to the floor. Both parents moved
to her . . . Rupert had gone to the head of the
　　staircase unobserved. He had his little
sword. There was a great crash —
　　　　　The door had given.

"Rupert!" cried Tanya, disengaging herself from
　　Alexei, whirling out the door in a
cloud of blue filminess, the boy stood poised,
　　his little jaw visible to Tanya and Alexei,
thrust out toward threateners of Escutonoff's
　　happiness, power and peace — Ccrrraccckk! —
　　　　　the shot

from a serf's gun rang out, the little one, the
　　Escutonoff fell forward, blood from his
chest darkening the staircase, he did not roll
　　so straight he fell, but his sword fell
rattling all the way down in the sudden soft
　　silence following the shot: Tanya's wail
rose, carried on the spasm of sound that broke
　　loose below, soldiers dying, Alexei had
picked him up, she was blinded with tears,
　　"Alexei," she kept moaning, "Alexei . . . !"

145

He seemed to be dragging her back, he tried to
    thrust her in the bedroom and lock them in,
but she could feel on him as on herself the
    hands that dug brown into the whiteness
of his sleeve . . .

            An army officer, a traitor!
Tanya spat over her shoulder, she fell to one side,
    the dead boy in her arms. "He doesn't know,"
she thought to herself deeply, consolingly, "He
    is out of the world, he is peaceful, he
does not know!"

            Then the man confronted her,
triumphant,

        "Countess Escutonoff, you are a prisoner
    of the Revolution, or should I say, my
prisoner, since I hope — indeed, I do — that you
    will consider me the lesser of the two
evils!"

    The fellow must be an imposter, obviously
the uniform was not his, but he was educated.
            He had righted her, little
Rupert still in her arms, his blood stain-
ing her dress. "Do you observe what I have in
    my arms, moujik?" she asked viciously. She felt
her burden violently wrested from her as she choked
    in her mingled grief and fury, attempting
to keep him— alas! it was Alexei she was thinking
    of already, the little one was dead . . .

        What had gone wrong? This,
surely, was only a dream . . .

Katerina, gone —
Alexei, where was
he?
His name died in her throat. "Alexei,"
her soul groaned.
"Do not kill him," she cried suddenly,
sharply, in a voice not to be disobeyed. "I will do
anything you say, Captain!"

Drunken howls sounded outside the
half-shut doors, shouts of exuberance, triumph, lustfulness . . .
"I will —"

"Save your breath, Countess," the Captain
said, steadying her. "I am not interested in
your husband. He is for — whoever wants his
carcass . . . "

There was a blank here

Tanya felt herself die down to her feet, and yet
remain upright, accepting the irresistible
arms of the man as he picked her up, instinctively
she sensed he was taking her to Alexei . . .
She seemed to swim down the stairs, recalling how
her father had carried her down stairs like
these as a little girl, she had shut her eyes, and
she did so now till she realized they were
downstairs in the great hallway, turning toward the
reception room, no, it was the library . . .

Shouts of derisive merriment greeted them
and the Captain set her down, keeping his arms
    about her waist

        She looked.

A little serf was at Alexei's throat, an insane
        comic fury convulsing his mongoloid face,
his rush had sent the Count against a huge
        table, on which was a globe of the earth
the blow of Alexei's back toppling the globe with
        a bang, sending it crashing to the floor
where it rolled over and over, back and forth dizzily
        in semi-circles, the serfs pointing and
laughing, Alexei's clothes were being dragged from
        him, the vicious little serf lunging
for gold braid at his chest, caught at his waist,
        the pants ripping, one legfront peeling from him
like the skin of a peach, the man's head, hard in
        Alexei's grasp, was boring against his stomach,
he was gasping, his grip slackened, the man dove
        for his throat, leaping on his chest like
a rat, bending him back . . .

        Black of memory was gathering
in Tanya's brain, so much that might have been was
skipped, she saw only what was, had been, some
dreadful fate, as though for this to happen, the world had to end,
for this to begin, the world
had to vanish in terror, under her eyes . . .

148

The gleeful chuckle of the pseudo Captain
came to her . . .
Now she was rocked in some terrible
convulsion as though the world had become
a ship at sea, prisoned in some frightful
storm, moving at some other will, being deprived of
its own . . . yet all clear, all as clear as
daylight in the flares and the still lighted chan-
delier in the hallway . . .

White surrounded by
black, nothing whiter than, now, her husband's flesh,
flesh of the right leg: closing her eyes, she
opened them once again, still the same vision, still
the same . . .

The serf leaped to the table
pulling the exhausted Count on it, his legs dangling
over, then another dropped his gun and rushed
over, dragging off Alexei's boots and with them
all the white remnant of his pants —
at which
a savage howl of joy went up, filling the mansion
with its detonation.

"Enough?" the Captain
said down her neck. She did not know what to say.
Of her own volition she could not move,
speak. Yet she could not look away. And she heard
the obscene suggestion, the last unbelievable
humiliation now intended for Alexei . . .

Her eyes closed. She felt herself
reeling backward into infinite nothing, realizing
     as the Captain's arms went about her and once more
she was lifted from the ground, her skirts drifting down,
     she would have to look once more . . .

          Alexei saw her,
bosom nude, swinging in the man's arms, her breasts
     rolling magnificently from their fleshy anchor
like things buoyed on an infinite ocean of air, the
     nipples following the outer points of movement
like markers obeying some unbelievably profound
     vibration . . .

       "Alexei," she breathed, and he heard.
Then she saw, sideways, but surely, the fountain head
     of her joy: inaccessible and nullified,
rendered a symbolic farce, the Count's
     masculinity drenched in a storm of sexlessness
but rising like an image from beneath water
     to visibility, a flaccid cemetery
of sex

Her head was whirled away from it, but she heard
       the serf's growl, "If not the Countess . . . "
And the intake of his breath, preparing for the lunge
     all the way from a corner of the room . . .
His lesser lust, inferior architecture, somehow
     triumphant, erect

        the perfume Alexei wore
coming to her even in this moment

wafted across space — or was it imagination?
the scented talc the Czarina gave them

It was real last night.

. . . And

Trembling in the same wind
the same heaving respiratory
Motion that shakes the world
the poet, blinded with being
does not explain
Nor escape implication
rushes
Rather, to it, being the medium
the rapt sibyl, yet
knowing so much —
And telling it all in a fashion —
hesitates to write the logical
dénouement
To so simple a story:

"She woke up, crying and shaking
her lover. 'Wake up! Darling!
Wake up!' "

From the depths of his being, he knew
she had awakened with the vision again,
that it was real, that it had been real,
that it had once happened to him"

. . . while crucified on the same
Wind, even, carried away from the
                spectacle of eternal
                      desire —
Knowing some satiety, some
                        completeness . . .
                Formulating
Answer to the Medusan vision:
                Apparition of the mother . . .
                "Mother!
Mother Medusa!
                    Close your eyes!"
        — life, a rag
                in the wind, the
                blindfold —
"Close your eyes —
                Perseus-Narcissus
His shield your mirror
                Truth
A stone in your guts
                Lie
Brought forth singing
                like a baby

        Sleep now!

        It is done."

Printed March 1972 in Santa Barbara
for the Black Sparrow Press by Noel Young.
Design by Barbara Martin. This edition is
limited to 1000 copies in paper wrappers;
200 hardcover copies numbered & signed by
the poet; & 26 presentation copies handbound
in boards by Earle Gray lettered & signed
by the poet.

The romantic portrait at the front of this book by
Pavel Tchelitchew is an essential image of the young
poet rather than a literal physical likeness of him
at the age of thirty-three. A poet's truest biography
is the history of his created forms and sensibility.
This comprehensive selection from Parker Tyler's
verse reveals his boldness, strength, and above all,
his vital expression of the substance of erotic
experience. His masterpiece, the long poem
"The Granite Butterfly," was celebrated by
William Carlos Williams and Kenneth Rexroth.
The other poems go to make up the total image of
a poet's life as hours and days, months and years,
make up the basic chronology of anyone's life.

Parker Tyler was born in New Orleans and spent most
of his youth in Chicago and Cleveland before settling
in New York City. There, with infrequent absences,
he has been (as he says) "close to life and death
for about forty years"; he expects to exist thus,
no matter where else, for some years to come.
Mr. Tyler is also widely known as one of America's
most distinguished film critics and as a notable art
biographer. In 1958 he received a Longview Award
for his poetry.